Loss, Grief,
and Bereavement

The Foundation of Thanatology Series, Volume 4

Other Volumes in the Series

Loss, Grief, and Bereavement

A Guide for Counseling

edited by

Otto S. Margolis
Howard C. Raether
Austin H. Kutscher
Samuel C. Klagsbrun
Eric Marcus
Vanderlyn R. Pine
and
Daniel J. Cherico

With the Assistance of
Lillian G. Kutscher

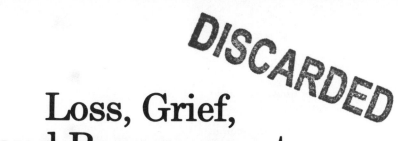

PRAEGER

PRAEGER SPECIAL STUDIES • PRAEGER SCIENTIFIC

New York • Philadelphia • Eastbourne, UK
Toronto • Hong Kong • Tokyo • Sydney

Library of Congress Cataloging-in-Publication Data
Main entry under title:

Loss, grief, and bereavement.

Includes index.
1. Death--Psychological aspects.   2. Loss
(Psychology)   3. Grief.   4.Bereavement--
Psychological aspects.   5. Counseling.
I. Margolis, Otto Schwarz.   II. Kutscher,
Lillian.
BF789.D4L67   1985   155.9'37   85-12260
ISBN 0-03-000489-6 (alk. paper)

Published in 1985 by Praeger Publishers
CBS Educational and Professional Publishing, a Division of CBS Inc.
521 Fifth Avenue, New York, NY 10175 USA

© 1985 by Praeger Publishers

56789 052 987654321

Printed in the United States of America on acid-free paper

INTERNATIONAL OFFICES

Orders from outside the United States should be sent to the appropriate address listed below. Orders from areas not listed below should be placed through CBS International Publishing, 383 Madison Ave., New York, NY 10175 USA

Australia, New Zealand
Holt Saunders, Pty, Ltd., 9 Waltham St., Artarmon, N.S.W. 2064, Sydney, Australia

Canada
Holt, Rinehart & Winston of Canada, 55 Horner Ave., Toronto, Ontario, Canada M8Z 4X6

Europe, the Middle East, & Africa
Holt Saunders, Ltd., 1 St. Anne's Road, Eastbourne, East Sussex, England BN21 3UN

Japan
Holt Saunders, Ltd., Ichibancho Central Building, 22-1 Ichibancho, 3rd Floor, Chiyodaku, Tokyo, Japan

Hong Kong, Southeast Asia
Holt Saunders Asia, Ltd., 10 Fl, Intercontinental Plaza, 94 Granville Road, Tsim Sha Tsui East, Kowloon, Hong Kong

Manuscript submissions should be sent to the Editorial Director, Praeger Publishers, 521 Fifth Avenue, New York, NY 10175 USA

Thanatology is a discipline whose focus is on the practice of supportive physical and emotional care for those who are life-threatened, with an equal concern exhibited for the well-being of their family members. Proposed is a philosophy of caregiving that reinforces alternative ways of enhancing the quality of life, that introduces methods of intervention on behalf of the emotional status of all involved, that fosters a more mature understanding of the dying process and the problems of separation, loss, bereavement, and grief.

The Editors wish to acknowledge the support and encouragement of the Foundation of Thanatology in the preparation of this book. All royalties from its sale are directly assigned to this not-for-profit, tax exempt, public, scientific and educational foundation.

Foreword

Grief is the emotional accompaniment to loss and bereavement and is translated into feelings and actions in a continuum that should be directed toward a restoration of the emotional balance that has sorrow on one end, the absence of pain in the middle, and pleasure on the other end. The reality of impending and final separation from a loved one, the impact of actual loss, and the trauma of bereavement impose burdens that alter the normal pattern of life. When adjustment to a new status quo must be made, interventions are required to assure functional transitions and the return to what can be called a new "normalcy" in life. However, when the quality of life is thusly diminished by loss and bereavement, grief work involves an accommodation to new patterns, new events, new relationships, and new roles. What is happening at the present and what will happen in the future must be perceived in a new context that permits grieving persons to adapt to the alterations in their family, social, and community situations. Resolution of grief and restoration of a positive structure for daily living are tasks that frequently require: at the minimum, guidance; or supportive intervention from workers in many disciplines who are knowledgeable in how, when, why, and what to offer in the way of help; or when required, therapy from psychiatrists and psychologists.

As the contributors to this book clearly indicate, those who can be helpful and therapeutic for the bereaved come from many disciplines and professions; their qualifications stem not only from their academic and professional achievements but also from their life experiences. Presented here are thoughts and observations from those who work as psychiatrists, psychologists, ministers, educators, sociologists, historians, consumer advocates, funeral service professionals, nurses, and financial advisors. They have all practiced what they "preach." Their own experiences of bereavement, in some instances, and their association with others who have endured loss, grief, and bereavement, in other instances, reinforce their credibility as caregivers and counselors who can guide the bereaved.

Chapters include discussions of the continuum of loss, grief, and bereavement from the time a potentially lethal disease is diagnosed through the periods of anticipatory grief, acute grief, and bereavement. The psychological aspects of dying and the psychosocial aspects of terminal care are analyzed; an overview of bereavement customs and behavior in different cultures provides a frame of reference for those problems encountered by the bereaved in contemporary society.

Perhaps, it is suggested, religious beliefs can ease the pain, anxiety, and fear of bereavement; or perhaps open communication about death can relieve anxieties and give life a new dimension.

Current issues in caring for the terminally ill and the bereaved are addressed, including the relief of intractable pain, euthanasia, the role of the funeral, and the practical planning involved in assuring some degree of financial stability for survivors. Also explored is the impact of loss on children, young adults, and the elderly and how these groups, at varying points of life's spectrum, can continue to enjoy growth and quality in living despite painful and sorrowful experiences.

Although failure to resolve grief can result in pathologies that are psychologic as well as somatic, appropriate counseling at the appropriate time can so ameliorate the trauma of loss and separation as to be of assistance to even the most sorely bereaved in working through grief. Whatever the emotional status of survivors when a loss is anticipated or when it actually occurs, it is possible for the counselor to give them a positive direction toward recovery from the pain of grief and toward a renewal of stability and fulfillment in living.

The Editors

Contents

Loss, Grief,
and Bereavement

Part I

Prologue

1

Dialogue: An Encounter with Loss, Grief, and Bereavement

Imelda Banuelos
and
Joanne LoGiudice

J: Loss is a common life process. Some losses are more
permanent than others, e.g., saying goodbye to children as
they leave for college is a more temporary loss than experiencing the loss of a loved one to death after long illness or
natural aging processes. Some losses have a more far-reaching
impact on the individuals involved. Each loss, however,
involves a period of immediate grief, a period of transition
and adjustment to the loss, and a period which heralds the
beginning of the next cycle in life.

I: Our focus is on only one kind of loss--the death of
a spouse after a long illness and the bereavement period
following death. I would like to share my experiences while
I faced the terminal illness of my husband, the painful
reality of his death, and the need to find a meaning in life
after his death. I've been a widow for two and a half years.
The ordeal actually started four months earlier than that,
when we heard from the surgeon that Freddie had terminal cancer.

J: During a period of loss, families may experience a
wide range of emotions: shock, anger, disbelief, depression,
hopelessness, and helplessness. The range of emotions is
broad and not all persons experience every emotion or experience them in the same sequence. It is important for family
members to maintain communication with each other and attempt
to share their feelings with each other and with other members
of their support system, e.g., clergy or other professionals
or friends. Will you share with us some of your feelings just
after your husband died?

I: Confusion! Mixed feelings! It was so painful to
feel his cold hand. However, it was a relief to know that he
was resting, that he was not suffering anymore. I did not
experience guilt, probably because our relationship had been

3

an open, honest one. Everything was said between us. We had
the opportunity to say goodbye in many different ways. However, he was gone, leaving me with all my confusion and mixed
feelings. This resulted in a numbness that allowed me to
take care of all the pressing matters and arrangements a
funeral requires. But the reality of this situation taught
me to see life in a different way. The fact that Freddie
died confronted me with my own death.

J: Any loss necessitates shifts in roles within the
family unit. During a long illness, patients may not be able
to fill all the roles they did when healthy (e.g., working
outside the home, primary child care, household chores), and
other family members need to assume these tasks and roles and
continue after the patient's death. Family members may feel
they lack the skills and competencies to fill those roles,
and additional stress may be created. For example, in a
household where the mother is a patient and where she had had
the tasks of primary child care and housekeeping chores, the
father, older children, or members of the extended family
may have to assume responsibilities that are new to them.
Indeed, the shift in roles may be one of the most difficult
aspects of the experience of loss. How did you cope with the
many tasks and responsibilities thrust upon you when Freddie
died?

I: I was fortunate to have Freddie's family. I was
helped by them according to their abilities. Some came with
me to arrange the funeral, some helped me to keep the financial matters in order. Of course, although Freddie's family
was all around and helping, they were grieving also. They
were suffering too. Sometimes, some of them could not bear
to come to the house because everything there reminded them
of Freddie. But I had to confront everything and deal with
simple things and big decisions. I could not avoid or escape
it. I had to make a decision about an autopsy. Permission
for an autopsy is difficult to grant when you have seen your
dear one suffer so much. I know now the doctors needed the
autopsy, but I couldn't give permission at that time. I also
had to make final decisions about the funeral and I had to
tell the children. I felt that it was my responsibility to
tell the children about Freddie's death. Since Freddie had
talked to them about his own death, it was easier for me.
But still, how painful it was!

Especially the first year after Freddie's death! Although they did well in school, the children came home so
often with headaches. They seemed accident prone too. We
went to the Emergency Room and some of the nurses said, "No,
please, not you again" because it seemed as if it was one
thing after another. Even to face the hospital again, now
with my children, was difficult but it had to be done. I
just had to go and face it.

The children also had fears and sometimes nightmares for a long time after Freddie's death. As I tried to deal with these situations, I came to realize that it was through the children that I could see the continuation of life and the meaning of life. After living with shock, anger, despair, and desperation, I feel that I reached a point where I saw death in a different way.

J: The final stress is the readjustment to life without the loved one. Time is needed for the grief process. There has been a dramatic disruption in the interpersonal relationships at home, school, or work and adjustments need to be made in social relationships. Support systems are especially critical at this time to help families cope with immediate grief reactions and the longer bereavement period—not just the first week after the funeral. What were some of the problems you faced and what was helpful to you during this period?

I: As I mentioned before, Freddie's illness and death created instability, a loss of harmony in our lives. There was disruption at home, at work, and school until I and the children could establish our "place" again. I have already mentioned some of the effects on the children and no doubt it was also reflected in my job too. It was especially difficult at home, though. It's like half of you is gone; your whole security is not there. Suddenly you come to an empty house, an empty table, an empty bed. It's so difficult to deal with practical, everyday things. Freddie and I shared the chores in the house, and suddenly, he was not there. It was up to me to deal with everything.

During this time, some community groups were helpful too. A support group for widows conducted by the hospital chaplain helped me. And finally, it just takes time—one year and longer for the acute pain to subside. Even now, there are difficult moments for me and for my children.

J: We have pointed out some of the difficulties families face during the illness and death of a family member by sharing some of the experiences of one woman, Imelda. We have focused on one small segment of what is a continuing process from time of initial diagnosis to the present. We hope this dialogue has given hope to others encountering loss, grief, and bereavement.

Part II

Facing the Continuum of Living and Dying

2

The Grief Continuum and the Alternation of Denial and Acceptance

Paul E. Irion

The word "continuum" carries two major themes: continuity and development. It is a way of saying that life builds on past experiences, that new ideas grow out of earlier thoughts. Dying and death and bereavement are not the same thing, but they have a great deal in common. What we know about one stage of the continuum informs us about the other stages.

In the past decade, we have seen an influx of professionals and astute volunteers into the activities of giving care to the dying and the bereaved. Many of these persons had their interest stimulated by or received training in the literature and curricula that have proliferated in recent years. These new entrants into the field of thanatology have often had a well-established conceptual framework before they began working with the dying and the grieving. There is nothing wrong with having such a framework so long as one constantly rests, re-enforces, or reshapes it on the basis of actual clinical experience. However, problems arise if the conceptual model is applied as a fixed orthodoxy. Instead of permitting the persons with whom one is working to inform, shape, and even correct one's theories, at times theories are used to screen productive encounters with patients. In some instances, value structures are imposed on patients to manipulate their behavior, at least superficially.

I would like to focus on a particular dimension of the inquiry into death and dying and its dialogue with clinical practice in any of the disciplines giving care to the dying and the grieving. I want to look particularly at the twin issues of the denial and the acceptance of death. All too often, we have operated on a theoretical base that acknowledges the normative nature of acceptance and the undesirability of denial and have not paid sufficient attention to the

ambivalence we note in dying persons or mourners with whom we
relate professionally.

One always has to make a careful distinction between the
work of a popular author and the way in which that work is
understood and applied by a broad readership. In 1969,
Elisabeth Kübler-Ross's book *On Death and Dying* was published.
We are all aware of her definition of five stages of dealing
with approaching death and of how deeply this work influenced
the thoughts and acts of professionals who work with the
terminally ill and the grieving. Several ideas stand out:

1. In the five stages, denial is the initial stage
   and acceptance is the ultimate stage. Using
   the implicit developmental paradigm, one is to
   think of denial as giving way to acceptance.

2. Denial, in its initial stages, is seen as being
   useful in two ways: it provides time for the
   mobilization of other defenses and supports hope
   until hope becomes realistically untenable.

3. Kübler-Ross is ambiguous about whether or not
   full acceptance is a possibility. She writes
   of "partial acceptance," of the inconceivability
   of acknowledging that one will have to face
   death, but she also implies that ideally one
   reaches the state of acceptance, especially very
   close to the end.

Most of us recall the rapid spread of Kübler-Ross's ideas
through many of the helping professions. This led to the
idea that the stages of death and dying exist, in the sense
of developmental stages: denial, anger, bargaining, depression, and acceptance were understood to follow one another
epigenetically, as naturally and inevitably as infancy, childhood, adolescence, adulthood, and senescence. Some of this was
explicit in Kübler-Ross, some was implicit, and some was the
result of oversimplification by her readers.

The consequences of this application of Kübler-Ross's
stages were: too ready categorization of patients, misinter-
pretation of what was understood as regression, and, most of
all, misunderstanding of the complexity of responses, particularly ambivalent responses. Even though Kübler-Ross had
written of partial acceptance, it was not regarded as valid
acceptance if any denial was present.

Four years after Kübler-Ross's book was published, another
important work captured the attention of a wide readership and
won a Pulitzer Prize: Ernst Becker's *The Denial of Death*. The
thesis of this outstanding work is that much significant human
behavior is motivated by a need to deny one's creatureliness,
i.e., one's mortality, and to defend oneself against the fear of
death.

Becker, too, in the end sees denial as destructive, although he stops short of a ringing affirmation of acceptance. He acknowledges denial as the common human experience, but he acknowledges it with regret.

> *The ironic thing about the narrowing down of*
> *neurosis is that the person seeks to avoid death,*
> *but he does it by killing off so much of himself*
> *and so large a spectrum of his action-world that*
> *he is actually isolating and diminishing himself*
> *and becomes as though dead. There is just no way*
> *for the living creature to avoid life and death,*
> *and it is probably poetic justice that if he tries*
> *too hard to do so, he destroys himself* [p. 181].

So we see in the writing of both Kübler-Ross and Becker that reality involves a mixture of denial and acceptance of mortality, but that both wish that it were not so--wish that the person could be accepting of death. Isn't this true of all of us? We yearn for absolutes, for perfection, for wholes --and they evade us. We are forced to be satisfied with the partial, the ambiguous. This is also true of our responses to death and loss.

The concept of bereavement can be expanded to a broader spectrum of experiences of loss. Humans can be adaptive, can assimilate reality into the existing structure and avoid reorganizing parts of the environment that cannot be assimilated.

Think, for example, of the ambivalence we note in the dying and the bereaved. Dying persons may talk about their approaching death and at the same time be planning future activities. They may feel lonely and cut off and at the same time turn away from authentic offers of closeness and intimacy. Bereaved persons will alternately cherish and avoid things that remind them of their loved one. In all such things, we see the presence of two simultaneous thrusts--to hold on to as much of the past as possible, thus minimizing the loss, and to accept the loss and begin to make a new life.

In admitting the ambivalence of denial and acceptance in the dying, we are still left with the conviction that denial ought to give way to acceptance. Or, to put it another way, even though we can see that denial serves some useful functions for the person facing death, we also know from clinical experience that too much denial is counterproductive. The question then becomes, what is the dividing line between denial that serves a useful purpose and that which is a disservice?

I would like to suggest ways in which that dividing line can be drawn in each instance, because the line is relative to individual circumstances, time, and resources. First, we

have to look at the person's level of functioning--not only
such objective factors as mobility, and the ability to care
for oneself, but also the subjective dimensions of what the
individual regards as reasonably satisfactory and effective
functioning. Second, time has a bearing on the drawing of
this line. The closer the person is to death, the less
effective denial may become. This is largely a matter of
predictability. The closer death comes, the more predictable
the time of death. Gradually, the uncertainty of the time of
death erodes, the process of denial becomes both necessary and
less possible. Third, I suggest that the presence of hope
that is not unreasonable also affects when the line is drawn.
Hope, even though it is based on very slim odds, is a powerful
force. There is nothing wrong with hope that a remission may
occur, that a treatment will prove effective, or even that a
miracle will occur, that somehow death may be postponed or
overcome. But, like the inevitable running out of time, we
also see a running out of hope in the very late stages of
terminal illness--often a prelude to the act of dying. In
summary, denial may be necessary and understandable when it
dissolves the ambivalence, neutralizes the effective level of
acceptances.

Now, let us examine this same dynamic in the situation
of bereavement, because we are dealing here with a continuum.
Those who work with the grieving are familiar with the struggle
to accept and the impulse to deny the death of a loved one.
Except for the most bizarre pathological responses, we are not
thinking of accepting or denying the historical fact of a
person's death, but the implications of that death for the
mourners: what the death really means--in the fullest sense
of the word--to the bereaved.

After a death has taken place, a number of social processes are activated that assist in the acceptance of reality.
Most of these are ways in which the living begin to separate
themselves from the presence of the person who has died. One
of the primary elements of accepting this loss is to separate
the body of the dead from the community of the living. Lloyd
Warner, in his definitive study, *The Family of God* (Yale
University Press, 1961), uses the twin metaphors of the City
of the Living and the City of the Dead. The body of the one
who has died is removed from the place of death, prepared in
a way related only to dead bodies, is the center of a social/
religious rite (the funeral), and is visually and then spa-
tially separated from the mourners after a limited time period
by burial or cremation. In most cultures, even those vastly
different from our own, the process is highly organized around
a number of structured personal and social behaviors. The
intent of these separation processes is to facilitate acceptance of the loss.

Another set of separation measures involves reordering
of the routine activities of daily life without the presence

of the one who has died. Being alone in the house, being
free from some responsibilities because of the absence of the
person, having to develop new patterns of decision making,
and, in many cases, having to return to employment are all
ways in which the acceptance of separation is aided and supported.

Other separation measures are taken through the social
and legal mechanisms for transferring property. These
measures include the informal process of passing on items
of valued personal property--watches, jewelry, and heirlooms
--to family members as well as the distribution of other
items, such as clothing, to strangers. Then there is the
protracted legal process of settling the estate of the
deceased. These activities are not only necessities for the
equitable and honest distribution of property to the mourners,
but are also strong social reinforcements for the process of
accepting the separation.

We must not be unmindful of the ambivalence of acceptance and denial during this period of early grief. In all
but a few instances, we see denial behaviors during this
period that are part of this process of moderating the impact
of the sudden, radical separation, so that mourners can
tolerate the massive disruption of their lives more effectively. The process of accepting separation through disposition of the body of the deceased is moderated in a variety of
ways. Even allowing for cultural and religious differences,
there are some special preparations of the dead body. The
body, in many instances, is prepared to be viewed in death,
not to create the illusion of life but to see the person for
a short period as he or she looked in life, a limited modification of the effect of death upon the bereaved. Only
gradually is contact with the deceased broken--speech and
movement end at the time of death, visual contact ends when
the body is placed in the grave or the crematory.

Denial is also involved in the processes of remembering.
There are many ways of retaining something of the deceased.
Keepsakes, pictures, mementos of experiences with the one who
has died--all remind us of the person. Mourners may seek the
person who has died, even have fleeting impressions of seeing
the person in a crowd or of hearing the person in familiar
settings. We do not erase by historical revisionism ones who
have died, as though they had never lived; instead, we stimulate memories of them in a variety of ways. More formal ways
of memorialization have the same function: tombstones and
plaques, college buildings with names, church or synagogue
windows; tangible reminders of the person who lived. Objec-
tively and phenomenologically viewed, religious beliefs that
conceptualize life after death or articulate a hope for
reunion with the deceased in some future life are also forms
of denial of the reality of death and its impact on the
living.

If we admit that in normal grief there is ambivalence between the need to accept the reality of loss and the need to deny (or moderate) loss, where do we draw the dividing line between effective function and dysfunction? We have to turn for our answer to behaviors of the grieving. Several features keep the kinds of denial just mentioned in relation to the balancing need to accept the loss. I suggest that a functioning balance of acceptance and denial enables a person to assimilate the sense of loss gradually, to explore the loss in unfolding dimensions a bit at a time. Dysfunctional denial is a static, rather than a diminishing defense. It works to undo the loss rather than to modify its impact.

Another dimension of the dividing line that helps us to determine when the ambivalence is tending toward dysfunction has to do with awareness. Functional denial can be increasingly rationalized. The mourner possesses sufficient strength to analyze and understand the process. This does not mean that denial mechanisms immediately cease, but that they are put in perspective. Dysfunctional denial requires the expense of considerable psychic energy to protect the delusion, with no understanding of the process. Energy that should be directed toward increasing acceptance is dissipated in defending denial.

A third way to draw the line between functional ambivalence and dysfunctional denial has to do with the way in which the mourner hopes. This might be described in terms of the direction of one's hope. Functional ambivalence maintains sufficient hope to struggle to adjust to loss, assuming that with the passage of time one will be better prepared to confront the loss more fully. The hope one has is dynamic, motivated to change the future. On the other hand, dysfunctional denial is based on a hope directed toward undoing the past rather than affecting the future. It requires that one resist the passage of time in a futile effort to turn back the clock.

The role of the helping professional in this process is complex. One does not wish to originate or needlessly stimulate defensive denial. It is more appropriate to be aware of a mourner's need to struggle with the ambivalence of acceptance and denial, to offer understanding of the need to deny while supporting the need to accept. Another way of conceptualizing the role of the helper is to think of the possibility of slowly but steadily raising the line that divides functional ambivalence from dysfunctional denial. We recognize that in normal grief it is legitimate to expect that the line that defines functional ambivalence will move upward toward increasing acceptance without complete dissolution of denial. As helpers, then, we are challenged to accept the reality of some continuing denial rather than to force upon mourners an unrealistic expectation of absolute acceptance.

REFERENCES

Becker, E. *The Denial of Death*. New York: Free Press, 1973.

Kübler-Ross, E. *On Death and Dying*. New York: Macmillan, 1969.

Warner, L. *The Family of God*. New Haven: Yale University Press, 1961.

3

The Psychology of Dying: A Redefinition of the Five Stages

Arlene Seguine

> *To everything there is a season, and a time*
> *to every purpose under heaven:*
> *A time to be born, and a time to die;*
> *A time to plant, and a time to pluck up*
> *that which is planted . . .*
> *A time to weep, and a time to laugh;*
> *A time to mourn, and a time to dance;*
> *A time to get, and a time to lose;*
> *A time to keep, and a time to cast away;*
> *A time to love, and a time to hate;*
> *A time of war, and a time of peace. . . .*
>
> [Ecclesiastes 111, 1-10]

Man has always confronted the inevitability of death with a sense of fear heightened by feelings of ambivalence. On the one hand, natural curiosity motivates him to explore death's mystique; on the other hand, death's finality all too often curbs the desire for revelation. More particularly:

> *Different concepts of death . . . have a deep*
> *influence not only on the psychological state of*
> *dying people but also on the specific circumstances*
> *under which they leave this world. . . .*
> *All of the encounters with dying, death, and*
> *transcendence experienced in the rites of passage*
> *during the lifetime of an individual can be seen*
> *as profound and experiential training for the*
> *ultimate transition at the time of death* [Grof and Halifax 1978, pp. 2, 5].

No matter how many, or how long, the seasons of life are the paramount moment of truth at the moment of death--the final rite of passage from this world. No matter how long one lives, and despite the cause of death, the nature of death still largely remains phenomenal. Moreover, death has an existential dimension in the sense that it changes the individual's relationship with time and, therefore, his relationship with the world and his own history.

When viewed from a psychohistorical perspective, man's entire life cycle is punctuated by events of separation that serve as rehearsals for death. Phenomenologically speaking, the landscape between life and death presents the most crucial challenge of courage for the dying person. In view of this universal reality, it is essential to examine and continually reassess the sequence of psychological reactions the dying person experiences during the ultimate period of his earthly existence (Schulz 1978). Implicit is the need for closer scrutiny of the psychosocial care available to the dying patient (Garfield 1978).

Recognizing this, Kübler-Ross devised her five stages of dying (1969). Her psychological sequence of the dying patient's reaction to death is depicted as denial, anger, bargaining, depression, and acceptance. This range of reactions embraces a very individual process for each dying person. Because of inherent personal dynamics, it is important to differentiate each dying experience according to whether death comes suddenly or after a prolonged illness with a series of remissions and/or loss of body parts and function. Such an approach provides insight into the cause and effect relationship encountered in the face of death experiences (Bowers 1975). Although Kübler-Ross's continuum appears to be primarily one-dimensional, that is advancing forward from the onset of denial to the termination point of acceptance, this should not preclude the dynamics of a forward and backward flow that may become recurrent or even skip a stage, or ultimately cycle back over one or more stages of the paradigm. When viewed from such a multifaced perspective, the impact of death can become more fully comprehended by the patient, the family, and medical staff (Weisman 1972; Kastenbaum and Aisenberg 1972).

In addition to impending death eliciting a social organization of events, it also evokes a range of poignant emotions (Sudnow 1967). Moreover, the interfacing of these two sets of psychosocial dynamics influences the ability of the dying person's success in achieving a consummate death may depend more on the crucial psychological transitions experienced each of the five stages of dying as explicated by Kübler-Ross (1969, pp. 39, 50, 83-86, 112-13). Because the whole dying process involves the person in a fractured time frame, emotional reactions can become blurred or reorganized. Hence, the need for the added dimension of the revers-

Figure 3.1   The Five Stages of Dying Reorganized

THE DYING PROCESS

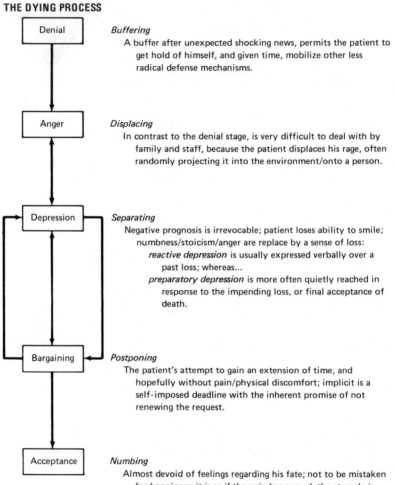

Buffering

A buffer after unexpected shocking news, permits the patient to get hold of himself, and given time, mobilize other less radical defense mechanisms.

Displacing

In contrast to the denial stage, is very difficult to deal with by family and staff, because the patient displaces his rage, often randomly projecting it into the environment/onto a person.

Separating

Negative prognosis is irrevocable; patient loses ability to smile; numbness/stoicism/anger are replace by a sense of loss:

reactive depression is usually expressed verbally over a past loss; whereas...

preparatory depression is more often quietly reached in response to the impending loss, or final acceptance of death.

Postponing

The patient's attempt to gain an extension of time, and hopefully without pain/physical discomfort; implicit is a self-imposed deadline with the inherent promise of not renewing the request.

Numbing

Almost devoid of feelings regarding his fate; not to be mistaken for happiness; it is as if the pain has ceased, the struggle is over, it is time for the final rest before the long journey.

Figure 3.2   The Psychology of Dying: The Five Stages
             Redefined

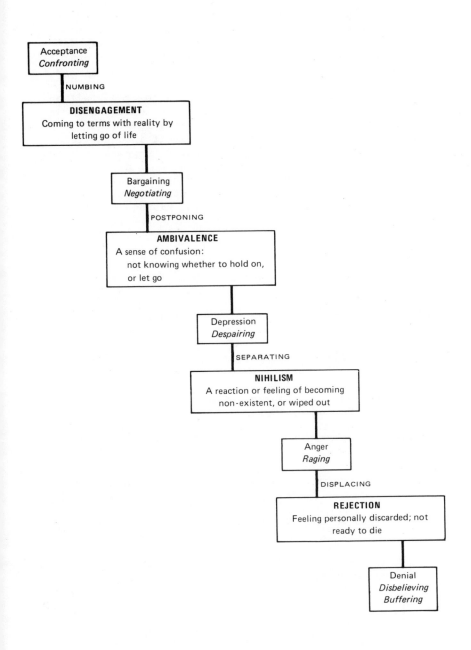

ibility between all stages, with the most mobility occurring between the stages of depression and bargaining (Figure 3.1).

The dying person is traumatized and confused by his fear of death. Since the anticipation of death is not a singular event, but rather an involvement in a sequential chain of emotions, fresh perceptions that acknowledge a wider spectrum of psychological parameters are needed. This concept is illustrated when one redefines the five stages with crucial transition periods--rejection, nihilism, ambivalence, and disengagement--interposed between the original stages (Figure 3.2).

Thus, the entire continuum depicted in the redefinition furnishes a more integrated chain reaction of emotional experiences with more latitude for the dying individual to continually reassess and reassimilate himself into the total dying process. In addition, this schematic suggests that the dying person progresses through a succession of psychological plateaus, which ultimately culminates in his reaching the level of acceptance, at which point he enters a new dimension in time while simultaneously transcending his own finitude.

REFERENCES

Bowers, M.K. *Counseling the Dying*. New York: Jason Aronson, 1975.

Garfield, C. *Psychosocial Care of the Dying Patient*. New York: McGraw-Hill, 1978.

Grof, S. and J. Halifax. *The Human Encounter with Death*. New York: E. P. Dutton, 1978.

Kastenbaum, R. and R. Aisenberg. *The Psychology of Death*. New York: Springer, 1972.

Kübler-Ross, E. *On Death and Dying*. New York: Macmillan, 1969.

Schulz, R. *The Psychology of Death, Dying, and Bereavement*. Reading, Mass.: Addison-Wesley, 1978.

Sudnow, D. *Passing On: The Social Organization of Dying*. Englewood Cliffs, N.J.: Prentice-Hall, 1967.

Weisman, A.D. *On Dying and Denying: A Psychiatric Study of Terminality*. New York: Human Sciences Press, 1972.

4

Anticipatory Grief: Two Case Studies with Unexpected Outcomes

Mahlon S. Hale

Two case vignettes that illustrate some of the problems inherent in the systematic management of anticipatory grief are presented here. In using the word "systematic," I mean that most of us who have witnessed the development of the numerous schemata designed to formalize the processes of grieving, dying, and bereavement look quite closely for familiar hallmarks and guideposts when caring for dying patients and their families, in spite of concerns that arise out of a lack of fit between what we expect and what we and our patients experience.

Staff expectations and treatment strategies are geared to anticipate formalized stages in the process of dying and in the accompanying attitudinal and affective changes expressed by patients who know they may or will die. This is not simply because an extensive and sometimes conflicting literature has made us aware of what to expect. Intuitively, we recognize that the developmental stages of attachment, separation, and loss used by Bowlby (1969) for his treatise on child development and the etiology of anxious behaviors in those who do not master these stages, are essential pieces of the life cycle that repeat themselves throughout the life span even as we die. The fact that we can now explain and clarify these experiences in formal ways is one means of reassuring both ourselves and our patients that we can deal with the anxiety generated by the uncertainty of the process of dying.

That process is, to my mind, most clearly at work during the period of anticipatory grief. There is a strong likelihood that other more subtle processes are at work as well. Unless one is morbidly predisposed to thoughts of death or, as we occasionally observe, a member of a family whose phenotypic expression includes a pattern of early death caused, for

example, by early myocardial infarctions in a family with a
consistent and probably genetic set of risk factors, anticipatory grief has a well-defined starting point. It is that
period in life described by Pattison (1977) as the "living-
dying interval." This is a point of life experience at which
individuals must confront a crisis of health; from this point,
their life trajectory undergoes substantial alteration. Its
rate of decline is determined by the intensity of the disease,
the biological state of the host, the density of supporting
life elements, the treatments given, and, of course, the
degree of tension that emerges out of the struggle between
the forces of certainty and uncertainty.

Elaboration of the formal schemes of dying superimposes
upon this downwardly turned trajectory a series of behaviors
or mental sets that are intended to describe the mechanisms
by which an individual comes to terms with this apparently
final alteration in life course. Whether caregivers resort
to Kübler-Ross's stages (1969) or Weisman's concept of phases
(1972) is less important than the fact that they are addressing themselves to the need to superimpose some terminal form
of organization upon a life process that sooner or later will
disorganize. In that respect, attention to the process of
dying and the anticipation of death extends throughout the
network of individuals who surround a dying person with a
sense of commonality--at least this is what we are taught,
and what many of us teach. But we all recognize that one of
the agendas for such organization is the binding of virtually
limitless anxiety. Yet what of the individual himself? It
is here I would argue that the idea of universality in the
dying process--or perhaps I should say that competing concepts
of that universality--begin to break down. Schematas are
clearly "goods"--that is, concepts of high moral value that
are maximally effective in the worlds of teaching and sensi-
tization. Yet we may need to be more tentative in our application of these "goods" to individuals whose life experiences
and expectations may be unknown or even hidden from us.

Perhaps there is no one way of placing in balance a
process about which we wish to make generalizations and individual life courses. We have to shoulder the consequence
that the widespread interest we have in the design or config-
uration of anticipatory grief leads to the inference that
individuals should fit some rule. To be sure, we have more
than one rule for those who may deviate from our expectations.
But the fact that we have rules and pathways--in short,
expectations--should also serve as an admonition that the
rules themselves may obfuscate what individual patients are
telling us.

We all know, for example, that some patients tell us
little, but do this in a way that leads us to psychological
speculation, based not on fact or observation, but on our own

interpretations of nonevents or, at best, events so impov-
erished of meaning that were they to occur to ourselves they
would claim the barest flicker of consciousness. These
occurrences, in fact, are relatively common. All of us have
seen relatively anonymous patients who have had relatively
anonymous life trajectories and quiet deaths. It should
therefore be no surprise that at the other end of the spectrum there are patients who tell us all kinds of things,
sometimes in quantity too vast to manage, sometimes in quality too difficult to interpret correctly. Just as we are at
risk in speculating about those who are too quiet, so are we
at risk in dealing with those patients who become imminently
central to our lives, whose bargaining and shifting attitudes
perplex us and violate the boundaries that we have designed
for the final pathways. Such factors took on substantial
importance in these two patients.

Mrs. U

The first patient was a 73-year-old widow, a retired
nurse who had returned to the Hartford area from her retirement home in Florida for a second opinion on a mass in her
abdomen. In Florida, she had been diagnosed as having a
tumor of the left kidney; this was confirmed by our hospital
urologist. At surgery, the patient was found to have a renal
cell carcinoma. A left nephrectomy and splenectomy was
undertaken successfully. Although the tumor was large, it
was encapsulated. It was the opinion of the urologist that
the patient had a reasonable life expectancy.

Initially, the patient did rather well following surgery. However, about ten days after her operation, she began
to have difficulty with pulmonary toilet. At this point,
she began to tell various nurses that she believed she had
an incurable carcinoma and would not leave the hospital. In
spite of increasing nursing attention, she became anorectic
and then developed cardiac arrhythmia, for which she was
transferred to the coronary care unit and digitalized. At
this point, her attending physician became increasingly concerned that her depressed mood would retard her convalescence
and therefore asked for psychiatric intervention.

We first visited this elderly, cachectic-looking woman
with a very sad expression in the presence of the hospital
chaplain, whom she had called to inform of her impending
death. To our surprise, the patient brightened perceptibly
as we proceeded with the interview, and freely told us that
she was firmly convinced that she had not been told the complete truth about her surgery. We explored this belief and
found that, in fact, it was less fixed than she asserted. In
subsequent interviews, the patient stated, however, that

beneath her concern about the carcinoma was a wish to die, which had been with her since the sudden death of her husband eight years previously. She admitted, in consequence, that there had been some mixed motivation for her agreeing to surgery. In addition, she had been highly ambivalent about her posthospital course. Her daughter-in-law later revealed that the patient had experienced intermittent depression while in Florida, and that several years earlier she had been treated with tranquilizers and antidepressants by one psychiatrist, with good results.

Our staff's assessment was that this woman was engaged in the process of anticipatory grief. Over the next week, we began to enter into intensive therapeutic negotiations with her in order to see what could be done to reverse her course and, in fact, to prevent premature death as a result of her depression. The cardiology section agreed to try a low-dose antidepressant. The patient was placed on a regimen of 10 mg of Sinequan, which appeared to brighten her spirits. Prior to receiving the Sinequan, the patient had made frequent requests for a series of pain medications. The staff had felt that this medication was not needed as often as she asked for it, and that her requests were manipulative. When her spirits improved, her requests for the pain medication diminished. Over the ensuing days, although the patient appeared less depressed, she manifested more attention-seeking behavior. Questions began to be raised about the degree of her dependency as a potentially chronic life style.

However, we then observed a resurgence of the patient's initial presentation. With every measurement pointing the other way, she began to insist that she was going to die. This behavior, which lasted for less than a day-and-a-half, included some food refusal, some pseudovomiting, and finally a morning comment to her nurse that she wished to die. At noon, she collapsed and could not be resuscitated. We could not obtain an autopsy.

Mr. L

The second patient was a 29-year-old single white man from a small Connecticut town. He had a 12-year history of systemic lupus erythematosis and because of his frequent hospitalizations for treatment was known to our service. Most of his other medical problems were related to chronic steroid therapy. These included hypertension, diabetes mellitus, septic hip necrosis, bilateral cataracts, and hyperlipidemia. Throughout his adult life, this man had never been in good health. However, in spite of his serious illness and its numerous complications, he managed a marginal existence on disability. During the past year, he had begun living with a young woman in his home town.

The patient's course became more complicated in April of
the past year when he was admitted at our hospital with an
acute inferior myocardial infarction (M.I.). Prior to his
hospitalization here, he had been admitted to his local hospital, reportedly had been cardioverted, and had been uncon-
scious for approximately 3-1/2 minutes. After ten days, the
patient was discharged from our hospital and was then followed
by our rheumatologists. He admitted to having significant
depression and repeated that he would prefer not to be resuscitated if he should experience another M.I. In addition, he
reported having nightmares after his hospitalization. He
described these nightmares as involving the feeling of suf-
focating, although he specifically denied that he was reliving
any of his resuscitation experience. He described that
experience in relatively familiar terms, stating that he
recalled his resuscitation effort and that during it, he had
felt that he was standing in the room looking down on the
activity that was being done to resuscitate him.

The patient continued to be followed in the Rheumatology
Clinic. Although his lupus was relatively quiescent, there
was increasing concern over his intermittent complaints of
further chest pain. In July, the patient experienced an
anginal attack while in the clinic and, under protest, was
admitted to the cardiac care unit with a diagnosis of sub-
endocardial infarction. Early in this hospitalization, the
medical staff considered the possibility of doing cardiac
angiography and eventual cardiac bypass surgery. The patient
expressed the wish to leave the hospital if that was to be
the therapeutic recommendation. He was then referred for a
psychiatric consult.

The psychiatric team found Mr. L in his usual mental
state about our service. He appeared angry and reactively
depressed without any of the neurovegetative signs of depression. Again, as with the patient previously discussed, we
sensed that the interview was dealing with a grief reaction
and that the patient's continued focus was on the loss of
control over his body. It was clear that he was past any
stage of denial and was into a period of anger. As the interview progressed, it was not clear that there would ever be
anything to bargain with. Almost immediately, the patient
detailed his history, adding as an aside that he knew it bored
us to see him for the fourth or fifth time. But he also said
that he had some new ideas regarding his medical care and that
he wanted us to help him obtain papers so that he could sign
his body over to our institution that very day. When we
replied that this gesture incorporated his mixed feelings
toward us, he rapidly agreed. He went on to say that he felt
he was getting consistently worse with each admission.
"Death," he said, "doesn't seem so bad compared with the way
I live now." He elaborated on this, saying that the loneliness his diseases inflicted on him, his physical infirmities,

and his dietary restrictions seemed to make life more painful than death. He felt that death couldn't be worse and said with a smile, clearly indicating a mixed affect, that giving his body to science would at least give him a purpose in death. The patient responded negatively to our discussion of angiography and possible bypass surgery, and he put forth the hope--again a double message--that perhaps going through these procedures would allow him to die more rapidly. He then amplified his mixed feelings, stating angrily that he felt separated from the staff and not attended to by them. We did not interpret this, but subsequently reflected on the total weight of these comments and recommended that the angiography be deferred. This met with considerable dis-agreement from the attending medical staff, but the result was that the patient was discharged without having had the angiography.

A consensus still has not been reached on this man, who is still alive three months after his discharge, and who returns to the medical clinic still enmeshed, we believe, in this process of mixed feeling stages. It is not clear if he complies at all with the recommended dietary restrictions, but he does appear to take some of his medications. He talks with us but refuses to make appointments to see one of our staff.

Just prior to his discharge, the patient told one of his nurses the following story: He imagined himself to be a giant balloon--a highly appropriate image, given his cushin-goid appearance. With each new complication in his condition, he felt as though more air were being blown into the balloon, so that one more breath might either wither the balloon or burst it. He added that he felt he was more likely to burst if he had to go through cardiac surgery.

A curious epiphenomenon of this case has been the patient's subsequent ability to maintain himself even while experiencing many of the characteristic affects of anticipa-tory grief and even while in a life phase that clearly represents the "living-dying interval." It seems that, like Mrs. U, he has somehow managed to make use of the process of anticipatory grief to preserve himself during this time.

Inasmuch as these cases reflect the unpredictability of our work and the substantial autonomy that our patients often maintain over their life events, even though we may wish to avoid it, some attention should be paid to our attitudes and reactions to these patients. With Mrs. U, the service began its efforts with much practical concern and very tentative hope. The patient was depressed and debili-tated. Even though the surgical and pathological reports were optimistic, we had some questions about the eventual manifestation of metastatic disease and validation of the patient's assertions. As treatment progressed, we became more engrossed with the potential for reversal. Our early concerns dropped away. Here was a woman who had pointed the bone at herself but who now smiled, ate, and chatted about death as an eventuality, but as an event more remote than she or we had believed. We were stunned and angered by her sudden death. It undercut the feelings of power and control we had used as reinforcers while our treatment progressed. We had, of course, forgotten or suppressed the patient's own prediction, her ready acknowledgment of anticipatory grief and, eventually, her apparent ability to fulfill that prediction.

Mr. L presented us with a different kind of issue. He quickly pointed out that his problem list was an insult to life, and so it seemed to be. Mr. L believed that his medical complaints were sufficient to carry a medical student through his entire undergraduate and graduate training. None of us was inclined to disagree. He wished to will his body to us as a final salute to our ineffectuality. Although we took what we thought was the humanitarian position with Mr. L and recommended against further procedures, neither we nor our medical colleagues perceived the many sides of humanity contested within this patient. We now suspect that we were relatively minor characters used by the patient in his own drama, his own experience of anticipatory grief, played out according to his own script, prepared so that he might maintain some control.

As with a group of patients once described by Weisman and Hackett (1961), these two patients entered the hospital with the anticipation that they would die. For Mrs. U, this predilection remained concealed until her postoperative convalescence became mired in behaviors that reflected her belief that she would die soon. Mr. L, known to the staff both for his chronic condition and the increasing certainty that he would die sooner rather than later, as one attendant put it, led to a different expression of anticipatory grief. His predilection to death was overt, not covert. His most recent hospitalization became a small drama in which recommendation after recommendation was debated and discarded. The patient took on the role of a judge, but we feel that he may have reached his decision before we could present our case.

One must conclude that the imprint of the individual upon anticipatory grief renders the progression and outcome of the process less than certain. There can be no doubt that the anticipation of grief exists. Its means of expression and its direction, however, remain open to question in certain cases. Anticipatory grief may become an unhappily effective force when death is not a certainty, but when premorbid elements, often unknown, intervene. As Engel has observed, the psychophysiologic substrate, combining uncertainty, arousal, and the activation of the fight-flight and conservation-withdrawal systems, predisposes to sudden death (1968). The imprint of these factors on our first patient is clear; they are less clear with respect to the second patient, but they are present like characters before their entrance onto the stage.

REFERENCES

Bowlby, J. *Attachment and Loss*. New York: Basic Books, 1969.

Engel, G.L. "A Life Setting Conducive to Illness: The Giving Up-Given Up Complex." *Bulletin of the Menninger Clinic* 32 (1968), 355-65.

Kübler-Ross, E. *On Death and Dying*. New York: Macmillan, 1969.

Pattison, E.M. *The Experience of Dying*. Englewood Cliffs, N.J.: Prentice-Hall, 1977.

Weisman, A.D. *On Dying and Denying*. New York: Basic Books, 1972.

--- and T. Hackett. "Prediction of Death: Death and Dying as a Psychiatric Problem." *Psychosomatic Medicine* 23 (1961), 232-56.

5

Unnecessary Terminal Pain—
An Obstacle to
the Grieving Process

Judith H. Quattlebaum
and
James T. Quattlebaum

Normal grief is characterized by both mental and physical pain according to Dr. David Peretz (1970, pp. 22-23), with "deep sorrow and painful regret, . . . dyspnea and deep sighing, 'lumps' or tight sensations in the throat, weakness, feelings of emptiness, exhaustion, decreased appetite, and insomnia, . . . anxiety and tension [and] guilt feelings"-- with the bereaved recalling "ways in which he failed the deceased: quarrels, disappointments, infidelities in thought or deed, negligence, impatience, and anger. . . . Any attempt to block or inhibit feelings and behavior related to bereavement may lead to serious maladaption to future relationships and future losses" (p. 35).

Citing a study by Lindemann (1944), Dr. Lyman Wynne (1975) states:

> *Failures of grief work can lead to a variety of serious disorders, medical as well as psychiatric. . . . Psychiatrists sometimes look for the consequences of grief only in the more obvious symptoms commonly associated with depression, such as sadness, crying, guilt, sleep disturbances, and anorexia. . . . However, well-controlled medical studies of nonpsychiatric populations have convincingly documented that there is a highly significant increase in mortality of close relatives. . . . Some patients have such severe losses and stresses in rapid succession that they become more enduringly incapacitated.*

According to Dr. Paul Huston (1975, p. 1045):

> *Most often in the first month of bereavement, anger appears in many of the bereaved as a fluc-*

tuating emotion. . . . [I]n an irascible mood,
the griever quarrels with friends and says they do
not understand his 'broken heart'; he charges
doctors and nurses with improper care of the spouse
during the terminal illness, and he reproaches
himself for not doing more to prevent the death.
Expression of anger may drive friends away, leading
to social isolation, loss of courage, and unhap-
piness.

This chapter raises some questions about the effect of inadequate treatment of pain upon the grief process. First, however, it must be made clear that inadequate treatment of pain is very common in United States medical management of terminal pain.

In a presentation to the International Symposium on Pain of Advanced Cancer, Dr. John J. Bonica (1979, pp. 8-9) stated: "All too frequently cancer pain is inadequately managed and, consequently, the patient ends his or her last weeks or even years of life in great discomfort, suffering, and disability which precludes 'a quality of life' that is vital to these patients."

Bonica cites figures of severe pain in up to 80 percent of patients with advanced cancer. In a study by Marks and Sachar (1973) it was concluded that not only did many physicians prescribe inadequate amounts of analgesics for cancer pain but also that most patients received only about 20 to 25 percent of the amount prescribed.

Orville Kelly, founder of "Make Today Count," an international self-help organization for people with life-threatening illness and their families, wrote that "Control of pain is probably the most important thing that can be done in making dying patients as comfortable as possible." He said that most patients he talked with expressed two fears --"pain and death," but that "fear of pain was more often discussed than fear of death" (1979, p. 235).

On the face of it, it appears that the kind of prolonged terminal agony that is the lot of some cancer patients who receive inadequate treatment might lead to serious complications in the grieving process of family members and friends (Rees and Lutkins 1967). To what extent is a patient's isolation increased when friends and family cannot bear seeing his agony? Must not their grieving then be affected subsequently? Is guilt intensified? Does denial of pain by the family affect subsequent grief or predispose to denial of grief? Does such denial complicate grieving in other ways? How is grieving affected when death is viewed as a merciful relief? How is anger at caregivers affected and handled when it is realistically justified?

Dr. Thomas Gonda (1970, p. 269) notes that "At times the bereaved has pain complaint very reminiscent of that of the dying, especially when there has been a close identification." To manage these pain complaints, the physician, according to Gonda, "must be able to reassure the survivor that all reasonable steps are being or have been taken to assist the dying."

Little else has been found in the literature about the effect of terminal agony on the grieving process. This is not surprising, in a way. While chronic pain is a very popular subject these days, terminal pain is an area from which much of American medicine turns its eyes.

The problem of false assurance of pain control with available drugs here in the United States was clearly demonstrated in the documentary of the story of Joan Robinson, a cancer victim, shown on public television a few years ago. Early in her illness, Joan Robinson asked her doctor if she should arrange to go to England, which she could easily do at the time with the help of her British husband, because she feared the possibility of unbearable pain and because in England heroin would be available. At that time, her doctor told her there was no need to worry. But later on, when it was too late to move to England, to the horror of her helpless family, she suffered unbearable agony in the terminal stages of her illness.

Dr. Avery Weisman (1968) says that he and Dr. Thomas Hackett introduced the term "appropriate death" to describe "what a dying person might have chosen for himself--had he a choice!" He gives the first criterion for "appropriate death" as "nothing more mysterious or arcane than the ability to control pain." Bonica emphasizes the high incidence of undertreatment because of inadequate knowledge of the pharmacology of analgesic drugs and to misconceptions among physicians, nurses, and other health professionals about the risk of addiction.

Our committee receives many letters from grieving relatives who write about the terrible suffering that was not adequately treated. Excerpts from these follow.

> *Lost my daughter from leukemia. I still hear her screams. I have a big mouth and much hatred inside. I fear nothing and nobody. I would shout on the streets in your behalf. (In recounting how the morphine "was to no avail," this mother said, "Many tears are falling. I best close.")*

> *. . . My husband died . . . of malignant melanoma at the age of 49. I suspect nightmares will be a permanent part of my night's restlessness. Whatever, whoever, I can write to, to add a "yes" for encouraging the ministering of heroin, or whatever, to relieve the agony of the patient, and the trauma and anguish of the survivors that never ceases as*

> *the mind replays the suffering of one that is*
> *loved so deeply. The scars can never be erased.*
>
> *I'm sure I am only one of many who saw nothing*
> *routine about my husband's suffering an agony of*
> *pain when morphine wasn't effective. . . . This*
> *is another obscene manifestation of a painkiller*
> *that doesn't work. . . . Why, the doctors assured*
> *me, they could keep him . . . reasonably free of*
> *pain! There is nothing reasonable about the pain*
> *of a patient who is terminally ill with cancer*
> *. . . destroying a person before death.*

While Dr. Gonda did not specifically outline all the
reasonable steps to be taken to assist the dying and reassure
the survivor, we would certainly have to include adequate
prevention and control of pain in the dying as being of primary importance. Such reassurance cannot be accepted as
believable when we deny essential analgesics for some dying
Americans.

For example, we know that 80 years of clinical experience in England has found heroin to be indispensable for some
cases of pain in advanced cancer. In the United States, the
National Committee on the Treatment of Intractable Pain is
pressing for an ideal in the advancement of better pain con-
trol--particularly pain that is beyond the control of available drugs and conventional techniques. No serious war on
pain can ignore the importance of any effective analgesic as
part of the program. That is why our push for a positive,
innovative, and aggressive approach to the treatment of pain
includes, as one practical and symbolic first step, making
heroin available--when medically indicated--for pain in
advanced cancer. The "fear of addiction" referred to by
Bonica, has no place here, when we speak of the dying, in
particular.

Congress has yet to pass a bill that would allow heroin
to be prescribed for terminal cancer patients. We continue
to seek action that will give our population assurance that
we are doing all we can to alleviate the agonizing pain of
the dying. Complacency and denial are inappropriate to the
challenge before us: to destroy the horror of pain that now
haunts so many heavy hearts.

REFERENCES

Bonica, J.J. "Importance of the Problem." In J.J. Bonica
    and V. Ventafridda, eds., *Advances in Pain Research and
    Therapy*, Vol. 2, pp. 8-9. New York: Raven Press, 1979.

Gonda, T.A. "Pain and Addiction in Terminal Illness." In
    B. Schoenberg, A.C. Carr, D. Peretz, and A.H. Kutscher,
    eds., *Loss and Grief: Psychological Management in
    Medical Practice*, pp. 261-79. New York: Columbia
    University Press, 1970.

Huston, P.E. "Psychotic Depressive Reaction." In A.M.
    Freedman, H.I. Kaplan, and B.J. Sadock, eds., *Compre-
    hensive Textbook of Psychiatry*, Vol. 1, Chap. 18.
    Baltimore: Williams & Wilkins, 1975.

Kelly, O. *Until Tomorrow Comes*. New York: Everest House,
    1979.

Lindemann, E. "Symptomatology and Management of Acute Grief."
    American Journal of Psychiatry 101 (1944), 141.

Marks, R.M. and E.J. Sachar. "Undertreatment of Medical
    Inpatients with Narcotic Analgesics." *Annals of Internal
    Medicine* 78 (1973), 173-81.

Peretz, D. "Reaction to Loss." In B. Schoenberg, A.C. Carr,
    D. Peretz, and A.H. Kutscher, eds., *Loss and Grief:
    Psychological Management in Medical Practice*, pp. 20-35.
    New York: Columbia University Press, 1970.

Rees, W.R. and S. Lutkins. "Mortality of Bereavement."
    British Medical Journal 4 (1967), 13.

Weisman, A.D. "The Right Way to Die." *Psychiatry and Social
    Science Review* (a magazine of book reviews) 2 (December
    1968), 2-7.

Wynne, L.D. "Transient Situational Disturbances." In A.M.
    Freedman, H.I. Kaplan, and B.J. Sadock, eds., *Compre-
    hensive Textbook of Psychiatry*, Vol. 2, pp. 1614-15.
    Baltimore: Williams & Wilkins, 1975.

6

Euthanasia—A Death Warrant
or a Rite of Passage?

Arlene Seguine

*For thousands of years man was lord and master
of his death and the circumstances surrounding it.
Today that has ceased to be so. It used to be
understood and accepted that a man knew when he
was dying, whether he became spontaneously aware
of the fact or whether he had to be told. On the
other hand, sociology and psychology are supplying
the first signs that contemporary man is redis-
covering death* [Aries 1975, pp. 135-36].

*Only recently have we begun to see death as part
of the process of living, and to learn something of
the myriad of attitudes and responses to this
ultimate phase of life* [Gross et al. 1978, p. 150].

*And like all human situations, it has an
existential dimension--it changes the individual's
relationship with time, and, therefore, his
relationship with the world and his own history*
[de Beauvoir 1973].

Traditionally, our ambivalent feelings about death, that
is, our curiosity coupled with our fear in regard to its
mystique, have offered strong testimony to its enigmatic
nature. This theatre of experience is a universal one.

In the shadows between life and death, there is another
dimension in time where the ultimate challenge for contemporary man's courage exists, namely the meanings and the
parameters of euthanasia. This discussion will examine various kinds of euthanasia or induced death in relation to each
other, and attempt to offer an approach as a basis for probing
the natural interfacing between the dying person's and the

facilitator's points of view in regard to this action or
measure. Inherent is the need to question the current and
future implications of the so-called mercy killing issue
within a biophilosophical framework. Also necessary is an
investigation of this subject in terms of the sociocultural
factors that influence the decision of death by choice. In
fact, consciousness arousal about death in American society
has exposed a fresh perception of euthanasia as evidenced
by the relatively new phrase, the "life-death" cycle which
reflects an open recognition of this dual articulation in
life's continuum.

When considered biophilosophically, the themes of
euthanasia as a death warrant or as a rite of passage encom-
pass the critical question of who actually presides over
one's own death. Within an historical time frame:

> . . . the ancient meaning of euthanasia, from the
> Greek roots meaning a good death, changed through
> usage and the passage of time. Initially, it
> meant a good and easy death, and that is something
> that all of us want, no one wants a bad death.
> This meaning has changed so that now an alien
> element has been introduced, and it means a killing,
> it means producing death, it means inducing death
> [Espinosa 1977, p. 3].

Antithetical to this, but relating to a contemporary view,
Lifton and Olson (1974) have suggested that death is untimely
and premature no matter what the age of the individual and
that its acceptability relates to the psychological context
in which it occurs (Lifton and Olson 1974).

Nevertheless, within the purview of euthanasia there may
exist still undiscovered dynamics of dying. Implicit is the
notion of an uncharted biosphere enveloped by unknown para-
doxes of "life-in-death" existences, that creates not only
wider parameters of transfiguration, but also suggests new
interpretations of the active agent.

This is to suggest that there may be a metaphysical time
lag between the interfacing of life and death. In this context, euthanasia might, ironically, provide transcendence into
the dominion of suspended animation. Further investigation
along these lines may yield new insights into the phenomena of
body preservation, rendering today's concepts of mercy killing
either outmoded or shortsighted. This, in turn, requires that
we attend to our own consciousness-raising in terms of the
dying process, and our "intimacy with death" as Neale terms
it in his book, The Art of Dying (1973, p. 1).

More specifically, euthanasia can be divided into four
types: direct, indirect, voluntary, and involuntary (Espinosa
1977). Within this spectrum, the first option is considered

active or positive in the sense that it involves an act of
commission, or obvious assault on another person's viability.
Intrinsically related to this description is the following
precept:

> *There are occasions in which the patient's desire*
> *to live is undermined by suffering and disease*
> *even though his death is not imminent. Out of*
> *regard for his freedom over his own life and death,*
> *he should be allowed to choose to die by active*
> *means rather than to endure hopeless suffering.*
> *Furthermore, those who assist him should be freed*
> *from liability for his death. The moral distinc-*
> *tion between killing out of mercy and killing from*
> *malice constitutes a basis for distinguishing*
> *euthanasia from murder* [Wilson 1975, p. 184].

This last comment, of course, embodies the distinction between
euthanasia as a death warrant or euthanasia as a rite of passage. Furthermore: "For the good of 'society,' that is, to
protect every patient's [person's] right to live, the law
should treat active euthanasia as a felony except under legally
sanctioned circumstances" (Wilson 1975, p. 193). A pro-life
attitude such as this also endorses the biophilosophy: ". . .
the dying person [is] not to be deprived of his death, rather
he [is] to preside over it! Man [is] master of his life; he
should also be master of his death" (Moore 1975, p. 167).

    In the case of active, or direct, euthanasia the innate
question of responsibility looms large. This, in turn, invites
the need to recognize that in light of modern technological
interventions, the criteria for determining death may have to
be reassessed, and, it is to be hoped, within a more profoundly
humanistic context. Hinton has observed: "It seems a terrible
indictment that the main argument for euthanasia is that many
suffer unduly because there is a lack of preparation and provision for the total care of the dying" (Hinton 1967). And
Hendin has written:

> *Spirit versus medicine. The battle has been and*
> *will continue to be fought. Modern medicine has*
> *reached the point where control over disease is*
> *hardly questioned. . . . Each time a victory is*
> *gained, new ethical questions arise. Each advance*
> *in the capability of medicine increases the respon-*
> *sibility for decision making. . . . Now the resus-*
> *citators, kidney machines, artificial body parts,*
> *and the actual transplantation of organs from one*
> *human being to another force us to take responsibil-*
> *ity not only for the control of birth and the*
> *control of life, but also for the control of death*
> [Hendin 1973, p. 66].

This scenario poignantly illustrates the impending necessity
for cultivating a survival savvy commensurate with the
futuristic implications of life-in-death human embodiments
imposed by advances in biomedical technology. In a sense,
modern medicine, when viewed holistically, is undergoing its
own Renaissance. New definitions of death have been sought
and, in some cases, only tentatively reached. As a result:
"Euthanasia is a more urgent issue now that life may be
extended by medical science, simply because man is more subject to the prolongation of his pain" (Langone 1972, pp.
56-57).

The landscape between life and death may harbor still
another waystop for destiny's traveler: "A substantial body
of scientific scholarship has addressed itself to the evidence for life after death and concluded that the probabil-
ities rest in favor of it" (Greeley 1977, p. 70). The trip
ticket may be roundtrip with the destination marked to the
land of the frozen future. This may be a journey to a life-
in-death existence, culminating in a reanimated life experience: "Will you someday return to life long after your death?
That possibility is currently being explored through the
technology of cryonics--a discipline based on the principle
of cold storage of human bodies" (Landau 1977, p. 80). ". . .
cryonics confronts the problem of death squarely and ration-
ally, but few people are even interested in thinking about
death" (Hendin 1973, p. 170). This futuristic application
of euthanasia speaks to cryobiology--which preserves the body
in cold storage with the intent of attaining reanimation.
This technique of body preservation purports to hold the dead
person indefinitely until medical science has discovered the
cure for his fatal illness, when he will be thawed out to
enjoy a renewed life. This two-way excursion is, indeed, a
rite of passage determined by one's own volition. Such
"passengers" constitute a new breed of people known as "sus-
pendees," who will have chosen a newer version of voluntary
euthanasia. Too fantastic to be believable? Only time will
tell. Although cryonics offers hope of eternal life to its
"potential" citizens, or "resuscitees," there is no promise or
guarantee. Moreover, it is essential to note that:

> Unlike banks for frozen human spermatozoa, blood,
> and tissue culture cells, however, human body banks
> have not been qualified as "proven." That is to
> say, no frozen human body from such a bank has been
> thawed for evaluation of the functional and struc-
> tural integrity of its cells and for comparison of
> its condition after thawing with that at the time
> of freezing [Hendin 1973, p. 164].

Several cryonic life extension societies have been founded
nationwide and worldwide. The slogan of one is "Never Say Die,"

and its emblem is the Phoenix, symbol of immortality. In mythology, the Phoenix is a bird that transforms itself into a young being after 500 years by burning itself alive. It can rise again--young and beautiful--from its very own ashes. Whether or not cryonics will actually provide the re-entry back into this world remains unknown for the present. Yet the fact that many people have already undergone freeze-preservation may foreshadow a new generation of euthanasiacs who re-emerge in society in a different timeband. Ironically, such a phenomenon may prove that death is not the "lost" season, but rather a viable passage through time!

A more realistic way of addressing the problem has been expressed by Concern for Dying, Inc. (formerly the Euthanasia Society of America) in their credo:

- *Society must indicate convincingly that it wants physicians to be humanitarians as well as skilled technicians.*

- *Life-supportive measures should not be used to prolong dying in cases of terminal illness with intractable pain or irreversible brain damage.*

- *Medication should be given to the dying in sufficient quantity to eliminate pain, even if tending to shorten life.*

In conjunction with this, their program is designed to:

- *Promote free and open discussion of death and dying.*

- *Promote consideration of the responsible use of new powers created by advances in medical science.*

- *Make wide use of mass media, hold conferences, establish new chapters, and encourage study courses.*

- *Gather information; publish and distribute literature on euthanasia* [Landau 1977, p. 25].

It is their intent to preserve the dignity of human dying, while simultaneously establishing the parameters within which appropriate human authorities can give priority to advocacy of the sanctity of human life. Thus, the practitioners involved will have acknowledged, humanistically, their bio-ethical commitment to a fellow member of their very own universal brotherhood.

In his book, aptly titled, *Live Until You Die*, Miller comments: ". . . the tragedy or the victory of death is in the way one dies, not in the fact of death itself . . . [The]

recognition that human life has a limit is essential to
mastering the art of dying" (Miller 1973, p. 133). Relevant
to this is the reality that despite the astounding capacity
of modern bioscience to prolong human life, one incontro-
vertible truth still prevails: death is an unavoidable
eventuality for everyone. Indeed, this precept affirms the
a priori concept of man's existential dilemma:

> . . . that the essence of man is really his
> "paradoxical" nature, the fact that he is half
> animal and half symbolic. . . . We might call
> this existential paradox the condition of
> "individuality within finitude." Man has a
> symbolic identity that brings him sharply out of
> nature. He is a symbolic self, a creature with
> a name, a life history. He is a creator with a
> mind that soars out to speculate about atoms and
> infinity, who can place himself imaginatively
> at a point in space and contemplate bemusedly his
> own planet. This immense expansion, this dex-
> terity, this ethereality, . . . is the paradox:
> he is out of nature and hopelessly in it; he is
> dual, up in the stars and yet housed in a heart-
> pumping, breath-gasping body that once belonged
> to a fish and still carries the gillmarks to prove
> it. His body is a material fleshy casing that
> is alien to him in many ways--the strangest and
> most repugnant way being that it aches and bleeds
> and will decay and die. Man is literally split
> in two: he has an awareness of his own splendid
> uniqueness in that he sticks out of nature with a
> towering majesty, and yet he goes back into the
> ground a few feet in order to blindly and dumbly
> rot and disappear forever [Becker 1973, p. 26].

Given this conceptualization of finitude then, the question
of whether euthanasia is a death warrant or rite of passage
should still reside with the individuals who should exercise
freedom of choice to determine the time and place in accordance with their own conscience. Universally, the ethics of
euthanasia still endorse that:

> Direct euthanasia, the deliberate act of ending a
> suffering person's life, is not legally sanctioned
> in any civilized country.
>   [On the other hand], Acts of passive euthanasia,
> in which a doctor elects "not" to do something that
> might prolong life or a suffering patient refuses
> to take medicine that will maintain him, probably
> are more common and undoubtedly go on behind the

scenes more often than realized [Langone 1972,
pp. 56-57].

Indirect or passive euthanasia is more subtle. By comparison to active or direct mercy killing, it is a less
obvious attack upon human integrity. It is a killing by
omission. When considered in an other-than-medical context:

> *If a person is drowning, you do not hold him down,*
> *but rather you just limit yourself to not throwing*
> *the life-saving rope laying at your feet. This*
> *type of mercy killing should not be confused with*
> *not prolonging the act of dying in the terminal*
> *patient. Conscience may remain more at ease if no*
> *direct attack is made on the individual. This*
> *indirect euthanasia is the "allowing-to-die tech-*
> *nique," the "letting nature take its course"*
> [Espinosa 1977, p. 5].

Equally applicable would be the following circumstance:

> *The increasing ability of medicine to practice*
> *"spare-parts" surgery will put a premium on the*
> *rapid removal of organs from a body after death,*
> *but the doctor is subject to serious legal risk*
> *if the presence of death is not clear, since to*
> *hasten the death of anyone, even a person whose*
> *death is imminent, is still a homicide* [Lasagna
> 1968, p. 227].

In bioethical terms, the doctor is bound to preserve the
integrity of the person's life in terms of the multiple interfacing among the cognitive, affective, and psychomotor com-
ponents of human performance unless the individual elects to
extinguish his very own viability.

> *The life-death confrontation gives us moderns an*
> *opportunity to learn something of what the medieval*
> *writers called "ars moriendi," the art of dying*
> *well. This is an art that must be learned long*
> *before death, of course. In fact, properly speak-*
> *ing, it was for the medieval mind an education that*
> *goes on throughout the whole of one's life, to*
> *prepare for this last hour* [Oden 1976, p. 91].

However, preparation for this final event may well be
accelerated should the person choose the third form of
euthanasia, namely, voluntary, which is synonymous with
suicide. While the moment of death is almost always traumatic,
suicide seems to impose an added sting, often viewed as a stig-
ma by survivors and other observers:

> *[It] is usually associated with mental depression.*
> *Once the depression has been improved, the patient*
> *is no longer suicidal. In suicide the final door*
> *is closed and we isolate ourselves from the rest of*
> *the world. It is the final act of egotism, of not*
> *wanting to share self with anyone else. It is*
> *despair in its most irretrievable form. Most of*
> *all, it is the best example of lack of freedom of*
> *the individual. . . . Do not confuse suicide with*
> *martyrdom. In martyrdom death is caused by someone*
> *else, while the victim dies affirming life, and*
> *those high ideals which make life worth living*
> [Espinosa 1977, p. 4].

In electing suicide, the individual has chosen a form of euthanasia as a "right" of passage out of this world, since he no longer desires to engage in life's activities or is unable to cope with its complexities. A decision such as this, embracing as it does the antithesis of life, may suggest the ultimate expression of self-denial in terms of complete human maturation.

Somewhat related to this form of human extinction is the fourth kind of euthanasia known as involuntary in which someone else (or a committee) will choose for the person who is unable to take action because of an incapacitating condition. Euthanasia is never justifiable against a patient's wishes. Every measure should be taken to protect every person's (patient's) right to die and to preserve his right to live:

> *The law seeks to protect each person's right to*
> *live. Furthermore, it does not recognize mercy as*
> *a legitimate excuse or justification for homicide.*
> *Thus, there are no sanctions for active or passive*
> *euthanasia against a patient's will (involuntary*
> *euthanasia). Theoretically, in the absence of mit-*
> *igating circumstances, involuntary euthanasia is a*
> *felony.*
>
> *In addition to the right to life, the law guaran-*
> *tees personal autonomy so long as an individual's*
> *exercise of his freedom does not interfere with the*
> *rights or the freedom of others* [Wilson 1975, p.
> 191].

Unlike voluntary euthanasia, or suicide, involuntary mercy killing involves intervention by another person(s)--decision by proxy, which unless absolutely reflecting the victim's wishes, could either deliberately or inadvertently be executed as a masked death warrant.

In the process of probing the hidden dimensions of death, the universal enigma, perhaps a closer articulation among the medical, theological, and legal perceptions will evolve. This, of course, requires coming to grips with the whole issue of so-called mercy killing:

> American law appears in need of revision. However, some feel that legalized euthanasia would invite abuse. Any form of murder might be conveniently dubbed "mercy killing" by unscrupulous persons. In response, some euthanasia proponents have suggested that our legal system establish an evaluative body to judge which requests for a mercy killing are valid before the act is committed.
>
> However, some elements in society strongly oppose such measures. The major religions of the world are against euthanasia on the basis of the sanctity of life. They believe that no one should tamper with God's will.
>
> But euthanasia supporters point to the fact that antibiotics, kidney machines, blood transfusions and pacemakers already interfere with God's law. They also stress that the major religions have approved of capital punishment . . . They view the denial of a merciful death to someone who needs it and begs for it as hypocritical, and believe that the right to die is as valid as the right to live [Landau 1977, pp. 24-25].

The dichotomy expressed above suggests the need for a strong medicolegal approach, tempered by a theological orientation, in the quest for attaining a greater degree of resolution of this interdisciplinary topic.

REFERENCES

Aries, P. "The Reversal of Death: Changes in Attitudes to Death in Western Societies." In D.E. Standard, ed., *Death in America*. Philadelphia: University of Pennsylvania Press, 1975.

Becker, E. *The Denial of Death*. New York: Free Press, 1973.

de Beauvoir, S. *The Coming of Age*. New York: Warner Paperback Library, 1973.

Espinosa, J.D. "Euthanasia: What, How, and Why Not?" *Marriage and Family Newsletter* 8 (Spring 1977), 1-9.

Ettinger, R.C.W. *Prospect of Immortality*. New York: Doubleday, 1964.

Greeley, A.M. "Afterlife." *Skeptic* (March/April 1977), 70.

Gross, R., B. Ross, and S. Seidman. *The New World: Struggling for Decent Aging*. Garden City, N.Y.: Anchor Books, 1978.

Hendin, D. *Death as a Fact of Life*. New York: Warner Books, 1973.

Hinton, J. *Dying*. Baltimore: Penguin Books, 1967.

Landau, E. *Death: Everyone's Heritage*. New York: Julian Messner, Simon and Schuster, 1977.

Langone, J. *Death Is a Noun*. New York: Dell, 1972.

Lasagna, L. *Life, Death and the Doctor*. New York: Alfred A. Knopf, 1968.

Lifton, R.J. and E. Olson. *Living and Dying*. New York: Bantam Books, 1974.

Miller, R.C. *Live Until You Die*. Philadelphia: United Church Press, 1973.

Moore, D.J. "The Final and Grandest Act." *America* (September 27, 1975), 165-67.

Neale, R.E. *The Art of Dying*. New York: Harper and Row, 1973.

Oden, T.C. *Should Treatment be Terminated?* New York: Harper and Row, 1976.

Wilson, J.B. *Death by Decision: The Medical, Moral, and Legal Dilemmas of Euthanasia*. Philadelphia: Westminster Press, 1975.

Part III

Coping with Loss

7

A Historical Perspective on Bereavement

Virginia Montero Seplowin
and
Egilde Seravalli

Bereavement is an objective, social fact. It often involves a change in status: a child may have become an orphan; a spouse, a widow or widower.

Grief is the emotional response to loss. When people are grief-stricken, their total being is affected by the sorrow of loss.

Mourning is the way in which a bereaved person handles ultimate grief. It denotes a culturally defined style of expression.

When the loss of someone close is felt within a normal or optimum range of grief, the experience is followed by healing and peace in its wake, with social bonds permitted to replace the old one. This normal or optimum range of grief is predicated on the dependency needs of the mourner on the dead that give rise to the felt intensity of pain (Tobach 1970, p. 348). The loss of a significant other triggers the survival instincts of the living. Close bonding is manifested when one person has emotionally become part of another. The dead person may symbolize "ideas and feelings, special qualities and capacities" (Peretz 1970, p. 5). Death may bring about a shift in self-definition or role, status or style of life, present plans or future expectations, as well as loss of the emotional and material support these are felt to require. Death may symbolize the end of a phase or period of one's life (Peretz 1970, p. 5).

The rending of attachments produces anxiety, loneliness, depression, confusion, helplessness, fear, and rage. Such a challenge to the human defense system can cause regressive reactions. Childhood patterns of separation, with their accompanying sense of impotence, are rebuilt. Survivors' thought life, feeling states, and forms of relating are negatively affected.

Personal grief is also affected by the subgroup and the societal environment in which it occurs. Culture gives us cues for expressing ourselves, and in the youth-oriented culture of the United States, death is seen as an "alien intruder and enemy" (Zandee 1960, p. 1). The bereaved person is expected to recover from the pain of the loss quickly; mourning then tends to get short-circuited and ends prematurely. By the same token, the mourner often lacks confidence that the pain and suffering brought on by loss will ultimately diminish and be healed.

How can we, as a society, come to understand the meaning of death? A good place to begin might be in our collective past. History offers priceless knowledge and wisdom that can help to formulate new, more appropriate behavior. It is known that concepts and feelings about death are directly related to what is perceived and understood about the nature of life as well as the afterlife. Attitudes at death merely accentuate attitudes held throughout life.

Primitive people feared the dead. Their rituals concentrated on sending them on long journeys, and exorcising their ghosts from the community. Most societies had a definite mourning period with a precise end point, at which time the bereaved concluded their grief. Without the help of psychology, primitive people understood that the capacity to get on with their daily work depended on total acceptance of death. They recognized that unending grief meant living death, whereas completion of grieving meant healing and peace. Thus, the detailed rituals connected with death were directed toward the completion of the process of grief and the replacement of old social bonds with new ones, thus allowing the spirit of the dead loved one to go freely to the new abode.

The ancient Egyptians saw death as a moment of transition, a moment that signaled the beginning of a new voyage (de Lubicz 1967, p. 382). Death was considered necessary for the individual soul to reunite with the divine spirit. In fact, death fascinated them so intensely that their total economy, thinking, training, productivity, social and cultural organization revolved around the phasing out aspects of earthly life. The well-born entombed their dead with material comforts for the next life, such as food, artifacts, favorite animals, slaves, and even wives. The poor were disposed of differently. They were left in shallow graves or were thrown out on the bush to rot or be eaten by wild animals. Earlier, during their cannibalistic period, the Egyptians as well as many groups in the larger African society preferred being eaten by their friends rather than by the worms.

The Egyptians believed in one God, self-produced, self-existing, almighty and eternal, creator of all, and residing in all. He was assisted by lesser dieties, some of whom enjoyed enormous popularity. The cult of Osiris, for instance,

weaned the primitive Egyptians from cannibalism and taught
them to see divinity in human beings; it changed them from
roving nomads to sedentary farmers; it introduced them to the
concepts of incarnation, resurrection, and immortality
(Encyclopedia Britannica 1974, p. 736).

By 4,000 *B.C.* they had systematized the values of truth,
justice, and righteousness into their society. During the
Dynastic Period which lasted 4,000 years, the Egyptians
numbered four million, and their average life span was 25
years. The Egyptian *Book of the Dead*, their spiritual guide,
included invocations, rituals, and ceremonies intended to
facilitate the journey of the departed to the spirit life
(Evan-Wentz 1960, p. vii). The culture closely identified
the material and spiritual worlds; the hereafter was seen as
an extension of the physical world. Bereavement meant to
carry out rituals that were considered beneficial for the
departure of the dead toward their new living place.

Socrates was of the opinion that the living proceeded
from the dead, learning that came to him from the East. Down
through the ages, the yogin have made the same claim (Evan-
Wentz 1960, p. vii). The doctrine of pre-existence and
rebirth has been affirmed by the most enlightened in history
regardless of culture. Evan-Wentz, the brilliant translator
of the *I Ching* and *The Tibetan Book of the Dead*, states that
just because the left brain does not register certain ranges
of vibrations is no reason to reject concepts that esoteric
science and right brain genius have presented as underlying
truths (Evan-Wentz 1960, p. vii).

The Tibetan Book of the Dead taught the art of dying,
the art of transferring consciousness from one earthly plane
to other planes--an art still practiced in Tibet today. It
was a meditational guide that perceived death as a victory
rather than a defeat. Buddhists and Hindus still believe that
the last thoughts on earth determine the personality predis-
position in the next incarnation. For this reason the dying
process requires previous self-training or the direction of a
teacher, friend, or relative versed in the science of death.
Ancient Buddhic scriptures such as the Bhagavad Gita and the
Tibetan Dhammapada state that thoughts determine not only who
we are but also our destiny (Evan-Wentz 1960, p. viii).

As opposed to the Egyptians, Buddhists, and for that
matter Jews and Christians, made a distinction between the
material and the spiritual (Encyclopedia Britannica 1974, p.
735). As a result of this distinction, the priest, called
Extractor of the Conscious-Principle, commanded the spirit to
quit the body and its attachment to living relatives and goods
as soon as the person died. Relatives and friends, having
been notified of the death, gathered together at the house of
the deceased. There they were fed and lodged until the corpse
was buried. For as long as the entertaining of the mourners

continued, the spirit of the deceased was offered food which was placed in a bowl in front of the corpse. After the spirit of the deceased had extracted the subtle invisible essences, the food was thrown away. While these funeral rites were performed, the priests chanted to assist the spirit of the deceased to reach the Western Paradise.

In Tibet, every funeral was conducted in strict accordance with the directions given by the astrologer-lama who cast the death-horoscope based upon the moment of death of the deceased. He indicated who should touch and handle the corpse, who should carry it, and the form of the burial. The astrologer also announced what ceremonies were necessary to exorcise the dead-demon from the house of the dead, what special rituals were to be read for the benefit of the spirit of the deceased, the precautions necessary to secure a good rebirth to the spirit, and the country and family in which rebirth would occur.

The ambivalent attitude of many cultures toward death is reflected in the Jewish attitude toward the dead as being unclean. Their *Code of Hebrew Law* is an ancient encyclopedic compilation of instructions on every aspect imaginable related to the last confession, death, burial, and mourning of the survivors (Caro n.d.). While the Jews believe in a soul, the major concerns of the Code were practical rules and regulations to guide behavior in the wide variety of circumstances in which death takes place. With rare exceptions, the Code was followed even by such ancient prophets as Joshua, Saul, Jeremiah, and David. It also included scholarly commentaries that explained the subtler meanings of the rules. The Code concerned itself with externalities, with the physical world realities. It highlighted the human web of existence, the symbiosis of relationships, and it conveyed the idea that death of any one individual touched the whole community.

History has shown that the living experiences of a group serve to modify their thoughts on the afterlife (Toynbee 1970, p. 14). Changes are introduced that may pass unnoticed or, as in more modern times, be perceived more quickly. For instance, the Etruscan civilization which preceded the Roman Empire was obsessed with death (Toynbee 1970, p. 17). In time, interest in the afterlife dwindled and the process of dying itself was stressed. Those aspects related to the rupture of the soul from the body, the grief felt by the living in parting with the dead, and the moral character of the moribund became important themes. The body was displayed and coffin sculpture reached a high state of development. Professional mourners were hired; musicians, burial carts, and walking processions accompanied the sarcophagus.

The early Romans inherited these practices. Inhumation-- burial in the ground--was replaced by cremation. Burning the corpse had been introduced to the West by the Greeks in 1,000

B.C., who burned their war heroes right on the battlefield. Later, cremation became a symbol of status. However, by 100 *A.D.* lumber became scarce and the association with paganism did away with the practice (Encyclopedia Britannica 1974, p. 740). Greek philosophy, still influential in the Roman Empire at this time, had taught that the soul, being material, was dispersed at death. Another popular belief was that the Universal life force absorbed individual consciousness into the whole. In time, Romans also believed in individual bliss in the hereafter. During the first centuries *A.D.*, there was much speculation as to where the dead went after life. Literature deepened an ethical sense and the groups under Roman aegis began to believe that the terror of death might be mitigated by a righteous life. This included orderly habits, the practice of virtue, productivity, and membership in a cult.

These values were ripe for emerging Christianity which brought back the concepts of resurrection and reincarnation. Since prehistoric times resurrection and new life were connected with death. The primitive observed this repetitious cycle in all of nature. The crucifixion of Jesus dramatized death and the need for good deeds in life so that the spirit might triumph. Heretofore, while most societies undertook burying their paupers and those who were alienated from society at large as a responsibility, the early Christians rejoiced in this as an opportunity to serve. Death, particularly martyrdom, was seen as the portal to an eternal spiritual life. In fact, the new desire to bury their dead near fallen martyrs in the suburbs conflicted with Roman law (Aries 1974, pp. 14-18). Basilicas, built over these revered entombments, soon brought the living and the dead together--a condition that the ancients had shunned by promulgating laws for the burial of the dead outside their city limits.

During the Middle Ages, death was welcomed. Being caught unprepared for it was feared (Aries 1974, p. 4). A knowledge of impending death allowed for a ritualized ending to life. Intimacy grew between the quick and the dead so that in 1231, the Church Council of Rouen forbade dancing in the cemeteries, and in 1405 forbade gamblers, entertaining troupes, and charlatans from "doing their thing" there (Aries 1974, p. 24). By the eighteenth century, dying in the presence of a crowd of family and friends became commonplace. No one was too young to be excluded. Burials now took place in the Church grounds which were in the center of towns and cities. These events corrupted the old belief in a virtuous life. A good death--with an earnest last confession--outweighed a moral life, an attitude that has prevailed into the twentieth century (Aries 1974, pp. 38-39).

The industrial impact of the nineteenth and twentieth centuries, with its gearing of time to fit machine speed, saw a drastic change in the perception of death. Denial replaced acceptance, strangers replaced hearth and family, and a hushed segregated manner replaced the open social event. Interestingly, the ancient concern with funeral art waned for some 900 years. Then, in the thirteenth century, anonymity at the graveyard began to give way to sculptural and pictorial likenesses honoring the illustrious deceased (Aries 1974, p. 47). During that same period, small wall plaques also testified to the presence of a burial place. These simple inscriptions became increasingly numerous during the sixteenth, seventeenth, and eighteenth centuries. Concern for death of the self was their underlying theme. On the other hand, in the nineteenth and twentieth centuries, concern for death of the other person became the apparent theme (Aries 1974, p. 56). It led to a new interest in the accoutrements of death.

The study of cross-cultural bereavement is also suggested as a way of gaining perspective on the meaning of death and the expression of bereavement, grief, and mourning. One comparison of ancient and contemporary cultures concluded that death, not life, was the focus of existence and that the psychopathology of a civilization reflected its attitudes toward death. It also indicated that there was a kaleidoscopic variety in mourning throughout the world (Anderson 1965). These differences show striking and persistent changes in mourning patterns and the disposal of the dead. Whether the dead were buried above or under the ground, placed in water, exposed to air, or burned, resulted not only from religious, societal, and cultural dictates, but also from geography, environment, and climate. Inhumation has been practiced since the Paleolithic Age, and is the most universal method of disposing of the dead (Encyclopedia Britannica 1974, p. 738). Graves ranged from shallow dugouts to intricate subterranean palaces. In above-the-ground burials, small stone mounds were piled up by the Eskimos, while huge barrows were preferred by the ancient Norsemen. The early Hebrews used rudimentary caves, the origins of mausoleums and crypts, while the Egyptians built complex stone pyramids. The Indians and Mongolians preferred trees and platforms for cremation, while the South Pacific cultures used water-drifting canoes and rafts. Cremation in the West has had cyclic popularity. Although not taboo to early Christians, the practice of cremation waned in Europe except in times of crisis, such as during the Black Death. The incineration of millions in Nazi concentration camps during World War II blunted the desire for cremation. Since that time, particularly in the United States, shortage of urban space and concern for hygiene have increased interest in this practice.

The position of the body also varied. The early primitives folded the body into a fetal position. Later when the body was extended, the Muslims laid it on the right side and facing Mecca; the Buddhists had the head face the north; the ancient Egyptians faced west; and the Jews faced east toward Jerusalem (Encyclopedia Britannica 1974, p. 738).

When ancient and contemporary cultures are compared, it is discovered that the meaning of bereavement, grief, and mourning has changed. Bereavement, once necessary for the deceased in order to be accepted by the society of the dead, is now a concern for the survivor in order to be accepted by the society of the living. The old cultures absorbed the process of bereavement in rituals devoted exclusively for the benefit of the dead person that freed the family and the community from sorrow, guilt, or confusion. Moreover, mourners, having ritualized and generalized the transition of death, were enabled to detach themselves from the deceased and experience reintegration into the social group with the new status. Thus, these complex rituals encouraged the expression of deep feelings, with support of the community and opened the way for a healthy healing to take place.

To conclude, history gives us insight into understanding the meaning of death in our society, teaches that observances and ceremonies connected with death are time-proven cultural expressions that facilitate griefwork and mourning and support survivors as they restructure their lives.

REFERENCES

Anderson, B.G. "Bereavement as a Subject of Cross-Cultural Inquiry." *Anthropological Quarterly* 38 (1965), 183.

Aries, P. *Western Attitudes Toward Death.* Baltimore: The Johns Hopkins University Press, 1974.

Caro, J.R. *Code of Hebrew Law.* Shulhan-Aruk, no date.

de Lubicz, I.S. *Her-Bak, Egyptian Initiate.* New York: Inner Tradition International, 1967.

Encyclopedia Britannica. "Attitudes Toward Death." 1974.

Evan-Wentz, W.Y. *The Tibetan Book of the Dead.* New York: Oxford Press, 1960.

Peretz, D. "Development, Object-Relations and Loss." In B. Schoenberg, A.C. Carr, D. Peretz, and A.H. Kutscher, eds., *Loss and Grief: Psychological Management in Medical Practice*, p. 5. New York: Columbia University Press, 1970.

Tobach, E. "Notes on the Comparative Psychology of Grief."
    In B. Schoenberg, A.C. Carr, D. Peretz, and A.H.
    Kutscher, eds., *Loss and Grief: Psychological Management
    in Medical Practice*, p. 348. New York: Columbia Uni-
    versity Press, 1970.

Toynbee, J.M.C. *Death and Burial in the Roman World.*
    Ithaca, N.Y.: Cornell University Press, 1970.

Zandee, T.D. *Death is an Enemy.* Leiden, Netherlands: E. J.
    Brill, 1960.

8

Possible Failure of Immunosurveillance System: Grief and Cancer

Jerome F. Fredrick

Prometheus,
Prometheus hanging upon Caucasus,
Look upon the visage
Of yonder vulture:
Is it not thy face,
Prometheus?

[Aeschylus, *Prometheus Bound*]

The possible intimate relationship between the neoplastic process and stress resulting from bereavement has been reviewed by Fredrick (1971, 1977, 1981, 1983). The appearance of "cancer" after an intense loss experience, with its resulting grief state, has been reported too often to be mere coincidence (Holden 1978).

There is little doubt that grief is a nonspecific stressor that acts on the pituitary-adrenal axis. As first formulated by Selye (1952), the "alarm" reaction causes the release of above-normal quantities of the adrenocorticotrophin hormone (ACTH) from the hypophysis. This, in turn, results in stimulation of the adrenal cortex and thereby, the hypersecretion of corticosteroids by this endocrine gland.

Normally, there would be a biofeedback regulation of the ACTH secretion. It has been shown that this feedback regulation occurs via the blood corticosteroid level. However, the rapid or *reflex* ACTH secretory reactions to stress are relatively independent of the corticosteroid level; they can

*Supported by the Dodge Institute for Advanced Studies, Cambridge, Massachusetts 02140.

be only partly inhibited, and then by only large doses of corticosteroids in the blood (Schreiber 1974). Hence, it is not unusual that corticosteroid levels in stressed animals may reach titers of eighteen times the normal baseline secretory values, as reported by Riley (1975). In humans, the stress of bereavement has also been shown to raise the levels of circulating cortisol (Hamburg et al. 1974; Monjan and Collector 1977). What, then, are the consequences of this hypersecretion of corticosteroids caused by the stress of grief? These hormones are immunosuppressive. Therefore, the overall immune competence of the organism suffers. This immunosuppression caused by hypersecretion of corticosteroids potentiates bacterial, fungal, and viral diseases (Fredrick 1977). We wish specifically to examine this immunosuppression with regard to neoplasia.

One of the initial observations made by Selye (1973) in his elegant study of the alarm reaction of the General Adaptation Syndrome (GAS) was that the thymus gland, under the influence of the hypersecretion of corticoids by the adrenal cortex, underwent a process of involution. The thymus glands of stressed animals invariably showed intense atrophy. It has since been shown that the cytosol of thymocytes has specific receptor groups that bind cortisol (Claman 1972). Indeed, if as little as 0.6 mg/ml of cortisol was maintained in cultures of these thymus cells, no differentiation of the cells occurred (Charkravarty et al. 1975). The thymus gland is actually responsible for the construction of a "pool" of recirculating, long-lived lymphocytes of a special type, the T-lymphocytes. These immunocompetent lymphocytes have a major influence on the immunoresponsiveness of an individual. They are involved in all of the myriad reactions of cellular-mediated immunity. Such lymphocytes, derived from the thymus gland, call forth a wide range of host defenses, such as the inflammatory response, microbicidal action, kinin release, and, of extreme importance, phagocytosis (Lee et al. 1975).

The most important function of the mature, differentiated T-lymphocyte is probably that of surveillance (Santisteban and Dougherty 1954). This is specifically a result of the many antigen-binding propensities of this thymus-derived lymphocyte (Miller 1975). In its surveillance role, the T-lymphocyte is capable of detecting and causing the lysis and destruction of transformed cells, which may be the result of environmental factors, such as carcinogens or oncogenic viruses. These transformed cells may be described as "precancerous" in nature and, if detected by the T-lymphocytes, are usually destroyed by phagocytosis and lysed. There is little doubt that this process is standard operating procedure for the T-lymphocytes. If, therefore, these lymphocytes are immunocompetent, they form the first contact with precancerous cells and subsequently bring about their destruction. In this way, these cells form a vital part of the immune system, which guards the organism against the development of neoplasia.

There are many oncogenic passenger viruses belonging to the Herpes group. The Epstein-Barr virus is probably the most common of these. Its involvement in causing malignant changes has been documented and reviewed (Fredrick 1981). The fact that this virus is widely distributed in the human population can be seen by examining the statistic for antibodies to this virus: these antibodies have been detected in over 90 percent of people under the age of ten (Grace 1970). However, it is obvious that not all people who harbor the virus as a "passenger" are afflicted with malignant disease. It seems probable that the immune surveillance system keeps cells transformed by this virus in check.

Impairment in T-lymphocyte number or function has been reported by various investigators as resulting from hypersecretion of corticosteroids (Riley and Santisteban 1975; Selye 1946). A particular study using the mammary tumor virus of mice (MTV) is ideal for illustrating this multiphasic immune response. This study by Riley (1975) of the appearance of tumors in stressed mice is summarized in Table 8.1.

Table 8.1

Stress as a Factor in Mammary Tumors*

Group	Tumors at 400 Days (%)	Median Days for Development of Tumors	Stress
A	92	276	High
B	60	358	Moderate
C	7	566	Intermittent
D	0	800	Low

*Data adapted from Riley (1975).

The average length of time for the development of this cancer in mice is about 400 days. However, by exposing the mice to various degrees of stress, the tumor expression of the Bittner oncogenic virus can be hastened or prolonged. Riley correlated the findings with the levels of corticoster-

oids in the blood of these mice (Riley 1975) which, in turn,
were matched with the number of circulating T-lymphocytes in
the blood of these C3H mice (Riley 1975). In all cases,
there appeared to be a definite correlation between the
degree of stress and the titer of corticosterone. Moreover,
when the corticosterone levels were above normal, i.e., above
40 mg/ml, there was a decrease in the number of circulating
T-cells. In these mice, over 92 percent developed mammary
gland tumors within 400 days. On the other hand, when the
stress was minimal, corticosterone levels were more "normal"
as were the number of circulating T-lymphocytes. None of
these mice developed breast cancers within 400 days.

An earlier study by Muslin et al. (1966) indicated a
correlation between cancer of the breast in women and a
separation experience. However, in addition to a decrease
in the number of circulating T-lymphocytes, it is possible
for the grief experience to cause impairment in the activities or function of the T-lymphocytes. For example, in a
study of bereaved spouses, Bartrop et al. (1977) found the
T-lymphocyte function to be severely depressed. This impairment was noted at two weeks after bereavement and continued
for at least six weeks.

These particular studies involved oncogenic viruses.
Hence, the transformation of normal cells by these entities
obviously starts the neoplastic process. It seems probable
that the same mechanism applies whether normal cells are
transformed by oncogenic viruses or by carcinogenic substances
from the environment. The important immune response in all
these cases obviously depends on the recognition of the
transformed cell. This, in turn, is the function of the
thymus-derived lymphocytes. If the transformed cells are
picked up and destroyed by this surveillance system, then the
neoplastic process cannot proceed.

However, during the stress of grief, with its reported
hypersecretion of corticosteroids and the involuting effect
of these hormones on the thymus gland, it seems possible that
the number and/or function of the T-lymphocytes may be
diminished or impaired. If so, then a transformed cell may very
well serve as the focal point for the development of a cancer.

The "alarm" reaction, as postulated by Selye (1973), is
the first step in the triphasic GAS. During this phase,
hypersecretion of corticosteroids occurs, involution of the
thymus is started, and there is a decrease in both the number
and function of the thymus-derived surveillance lymphocytes.
The stresses that initiate these events may be of many different types, but the human organism has evolved an identical
method for dealing with them. It has been shown, particularly
during bereavement, that such changes occur (Fredrick 1977).
Hence, grief is undoubtedly a stressor.

For the system to return to normal, which is, in all
probability, the equivalent of the second stage or phase of

the GAS "adaptation" as formulated by Selye (1973)--the grief must be confronted and resolved. If not, then the final phase of the GAS, the "exhaustion" phase is encountered. This is the stage from which there is no return.

Why, then, cannot man turn off the system, which is obviously meant for survival, after it has accomplished its purpose? Richards (1963) has supplied the dimensions of the problem with regard to man:

> *If one looks at biology and biological species in*
> *the large, it is curious that the human should be*
> *so sensitive and subject to external events and*
> *torments by things that do not physically hurt.*
> *. . . Man is disturbed not by things themselves,*
> *but by his thoughts and fears concerning those*
> *things. . . . He cannot accept adversity. . . .*

There seems little doubt that the hormonal and reticulo-endothelial systems are involved in the mediation of psychological influences (Stein et al. 1976). For example, avoidance learning, or even confinement, is accompanied by the hypertrophy of the adrenals, by lymphocytopenia, thymus involution, and increased susceptibility to viral infection.

It is indeed man himself who, like Prometheus, is his own worst enemy: *"Look upon the visage of yonder vulture: Is it not thy face, Prometheus?"* The immune system will operate, indeed, through centuries of evolution, it has been adapted to operate for the survival of the human being. If the system is not impaired it will, as a consequence, protect against neoplasia. The successful resolution of stress, in the form of grief, will keep it unimpaired.

REFERENCES

Bartrop, R.W., L. Lazarus, E. Luckhurst, L.G. Kilch, and G.
    Penny. "Depressed Lymphocyte Function after Bereavement."
    Lancet 1 (1977), 834-39.

Charkravarty, A., L. Kubai, Y. Sidky, and R. Auerbach.
    "Hormone Levels in Immunological States." *Annals of the*
    New York Academy of Sciences 249 (1975), 34-42.

Claman, H.N. "Levels of Corticosteroids." *New England*
    Journal of Medicine 287 (1972), 388-90.

Fredrick, J.F. "Physiological Reactions Induced by Grief."
    Omega 2 (1971), 71-75.

---. "Grief as a Disease Process." *Omega* 7 (1977), 297-305.

---. "Biochemistry of Acute Grief with Regard to Neoplasia."
In O.S. Margolis, H.C. Raether, A.H. Kutscher, J.B.
Powers, I.B. Seeland, R. DeBellis, and D.J. Cherico, eds.,
Acute Grief: Counseling the Bereaved, pp. 111-17. New
York: Columbia University Press, 1981.

---. "Biochemistry of Bereavement: Possible Basis for
Chemotherapy?" *Omega* 13 (1983), 295-303.

Grace, J.T. "Studies on the Epstein-Barr Virus." *Annals of
the New York Academy of Sciences* 174 (1970), 946-66.

Hamburg, D.A., B.A. Hamburg, and J.D. Barchas. "Anger and
Depression in Perspective of Behavioral Biology." In
L. Levi, ed., *Emotions: Their Parameter and Measurement*,
pp. 232-38. New York: Raven Press, 1974.

Holden, C. "Endocrinology and Stress." *Science* 200 (1978),
1363-65.

Lee, K., R.E. Langman, V. Pactkau, and E. Diener. "The Effect
of Anti-Inflammatory Hormones in Immunity." *Cell
Immunology* 17 (1975), 405-10.

Miller, J.F. "The Immune Response." *Annals of the New York
Academy of Sciences* 249 (1975), 9-12.

Monjan, A.A. and M.I. Collector. "Stress Induced Modulation
of the Immune Response." *Science* 196 (1977), 307-8.

Muslin, H., K. Gyarfas, and W.J. Pieper. "Separation
Experience and Cancer of the Breast." *Annals of the New
York Academy of Sciences* 125 (1966), 802-6.

Richards, D.W. "Hormones of the Brain." In D.J. Ingle, ed.,
Life and Disease, pp. 387-400. New York: Basic Books,
1963.

Riley, V. "Mouse Mammary Tumors: Alteration of Incidence
with Stress." *Science* 189 (1975), 465-67.

--- and G.A. Santisteban. "Stress and Cancer." *Proceedings,
American Association for Cancer Research* 16 (1975), 152-
60.

Santisteban, G.A. and T.A. Dougherty. "Comparison of Influences of Adrenocortical Hormones on Growth and Involution
of Lymphatic Organs." *Endocrinology* 54 (1954), 130-46.

Schreiber, V. "Adenohypophosyl Hormones." In H.V. Rickenberg,
ed., *Biochemistry of the Hormones*, pp. 74-75. Baltimore:
University Park Press, 1974.

Selye, H. 1946. "The General Adaptation Syndrome and Disease of Adaptation." *Journal of Clinical Endocrinology* 6 (1946), 170-230.

---. *The Story of the Adaptation Syndrome*. Montreal: Acta, 1952.

---. "The Alarm Reaction." *American Scientist* 61 (1973), 692-96.

Stein, M., R.C. Schiavi, and M. Camerino. "Influence of Brain and Behavior on the Immune System." *Science* 191 (1976), 435-40.

9

Discussing Death with College Students: Its Effect on Anxiety

Robert M. Evans
and
Paul D. Cherulnik

The mainstream of research on death has centered on talking to terminally ill patients in an attempt to allow them to accept their own deaths. However, researchers have begun efforts to assess the attitudes of the general population to discover how death affects their lives. Various questionnaires have been developed for this purpose. For example, using the Collett-Lester Fear of Death Scale, Lester (1972) determined that females had a greater fear of their own deaths and the deaths of others than did males. However, females did not differ from males in other areas such as fear of others' dying or general fear of death. Therefore, Lester concluded that the high death anxiety in females may be only a result of specific areas of concern rather than a generalized fear. Pandey (1974-1975) used a 40-item questionnaire that indicated that males and females, both black and white, react similarly to death and that their reactions all have common elements of escape, depressive fear, mortality, and sarcasm.

Templer's (1970) Death Anxiety Scale (DAS) appears to be the most efficient instrument for assessing fear of death. Templer used a wide variety of procedures to determine the reliability and validity of this scale. A study by Templer and Dotson (1970) revealed no significant relationship between religious affiliation and DAS scores among college students. This lack of relationship was interpreted as indicating that religion has a restricted effect on the attitudes of most college students. Templer, Ruff, and Franks (1971) used the DAS and found no correlation between score and age for any group studied. However, that study determined that females had a higher death anxiety than males. In another study by Templer and Ruff (1971), females again had higher mean DAS scores than males.

A major assumption in past research has been that the topic of death produces a considerable amount of anxiety in people throughout our culture. This anxiety may stem from people failing to talk or think about death. Little consideration has been given to the effects of discussing death with populations other than the terminally ill. It seems reasonable to expect that discussing death would act as a catharsis for death anxiety. Therefore, in this present experiment, it was hypothesized that involving college students in discussions of death would reduce their general anxiety and death anxiety.

METHOD

Subjects

The subjects were 162 students, 90 females and 72 males, ranging in age from 17 to 65, with a mean age of 21. They were obtained from all class levels of a small liberal arts college. Seventy-seven subjects, 43 females and 34 males having a mean age of 23, were assigned to the experimental group. These subjects were obtained either by the experimenter, who personally solicited volunteers on campus, or through notices on bulletin boards, requesting volunteers. Eighty-five subjects, 47 females and 38 males having a mean age of 20, most of whom were volunteers from introductory psychology classes, were assigned to the control group. Most of the control subjects were given extra course credit for their participation.

Instruments

Subjects in the experimental group were told that the purpose of the experiment was to obtain people's attitudes on the subject of death. From three to seven subjects per session, with an average of five, met in a "bean-bag room" setting for a one-hour discussion. There were 16 sessions in all. The first author served as the experimenter throughout. The following instructions were given:

The purpose of this study is to determine people's attitudes concerning the subject of death. We feel the best way this can be accomplished is to have people discuss death. The handouts being distributed deal with death-related topics. Concern yourself with one question at a time. Read the questions carefully, read over every item; then

rate the item that applies to you the most by
inserting the number one by the item. After
everyone has rated the first question, we will
go around the room and have each person tell
which item he chose, and explain why he chose
the one he did. If at any time anyone wishes
to make a comment, agreement, or disagreement,
feel free to interject.

Discussions were allowed to follow their own course of
development. The experimenter in the group used a reflective
technique in the discussions. In this way, experimenter
influence was minimized. Immediately after the discussion
of all four questions, which took an average of 50 minutes,
subjects were administered the DAS and the State-Trait
Anxiety Inventory (STAI). The order in which these instruments were given was reversed for every 20 subjects. Standard instructions were given for both instruments. After
completion of these questionnaires, subjects were further
instructed to keep the group discussion confidential so that
the experimenter could treat each subsequent group in the
same manner.

Subjects in the control group were scheduled in two
classroom sessions to fill out their questionnaires. Subjects
were informed merely that completion of the questionnaires
was part of an experiment. These respondents were also given
standard instructions for the DAS and the STAI, which were
given in the same counterbalanced order used in the experimental group. Respondents were further requested to respond
to the discussion topics used for the experimental group by
choosing the items that best expressed the way they felt.
These students did not, however, participate in any type of
discussion. After completion of the instruments, subjects
simply departed from the room.

Results

Analysis of variance demonstrated a significant difference in DAS scores between the experimental and control
groups. Subjects who participated in discussions of death
had lower scores, $F (1,150) = 8.065$, $p < .005$. DAS means for
the experimental and control groups were 6.38 and 7.45,
respectively. Also, females in both groups had higher DAS
scores than did males, $F (1,150) = 4.103$, $p < .045$. The mean
DAS scores for men and women were 6.48 and 7.35, respectively.

A significant two-way interaction between group and sex
in the analysis of STAI scores showed that males in the
experimental group scored lower on state anxiety than males
in the control group, although there was no difference between

females in the two groups, $F(1,150) = 6,435$, $P < .012$. Finally, there were no significant differences in trait anxiety. Mean scores for the three measures of anxiety are shown in Table 9.1. Norms for college students are included for comparison.

DISCUSSION

As predicted, discussions of death led to a reduction of death anxiety in an undergraduate population, in addition to a lower level of state anxiety in males. Also, it was found that females had higher death anxiety than males, which supports results obtained by Lester (1972), Templer and Ruff (1971), and Templer, Ruff, and Franks (1971), who concluded: "It appears that death anxiety is not so much a fixed entity as a state that is sensitive to environmental events in general and to the impact of interpersonal relationships in particular." Their speculation appears to be correct since, in this study, the "environmental event" of discussing death reduced death anxiety in the experimental group.

In establishing norms for the STAI, Spielberger, Gorsuch, and Lushene (1970) concluded that "The A-State scale is evidently sensitive to the conditions under which the inventory is administered." This conclusion was also supported by this present investigation in that males in the experimental group obtained lower state anxiety scores than males in the control group. Furthermore, there was only a slight difference between the trait anxiety means of the two groups studied and between those means and the normative trait means of 37.68 for males and 38.25 for females. This consistency in trait anxiety means suggests that the experimental and control groups were comparable in their chronic level of anxiety.

It appears, then, that discussing death did act as a catharsis for death anxiety. However, this experiment did not determine whether the cathartic effect was temporary or permanent. Perhaps future experimenters could apply these instruments to subjects on a follow-up basis to determine any long-term effects. Murray (1974) has reported data suggesting that such a change can persist over a longer period, although her study was poorly controlled and the reduction in anxiety was inexplicably delayed until long after discussions had ended. It is also suggested that researchers might apply these instruments to students prior to and after enrollment in a Death and Dying course. Discussions of death might also play a role in psychotherapy as an additional means of reducing clients' anxiety. It is possible that allowing more outlets of death anxiety might allow our society to gain healthier perspectives on both life and death (Wilcox and Sutton 1977).

Table 9.1

Discussion Topics: What Aspect of Your Death
Is Most Distasteful

1. What aspect of your death is most distasteful to you?

_____ no longer have any experiences

_____ afraid of what might happen to my body after death

_____ uncertain as to what might happen to me if there
is a life after death

_____ could no longer provide for dependents

_____ it would cause grief to my relatives and friends

_____ all my plans and projects would come to an end

_____ the process of dying might be painful

_____ other

2. What does death mean to you?

_____ the end; the final process of life

_____ the beginning of life after death; a transition;
a new beginning

_____ a joining of the spirit with a universal consciousness

_____ a kind of endless sleep; rest and peace

_____ termination of life but with survival of the
spirit

_____ don't know

_____ other

3. If you had a choice, what kind of death would you prefer?

_____ tragic, violent death

_____ sudden, but not violent death

_____ quiet, dignified death

_____ death in the line of duty

_____ death after a great achievement

_____ suicide

_____ homicide victim

_____ there is no "appropriate" kind of death

_____ other

4. If you learned that you had a terminal disease and a limited time to live, how would you want to spend the time until you died?

_____ I would make a marked change in my lifestyle; satisfy hedonistic needs (travel, sex, drugs, etc.)

_____ I would become more withdrawn; reading, contemplating, or praying

_____ I would shift from a concern for my own needs to a concern for others (family or friends)

_____ I would attempt to complete projects; tie up loose ends

_____ make little or no change in life style

_____ try to do one very important thing

_____ consider suicide

_____ other

REFERENCES

Lester, D. "Studies in Death Attitudes." *Psychological Reports* 30:2 (1972), 440.

Murray, P. "Death Education and Its Effect on the Death Anxiety Level of Nurses." *Psychological Reports* 35 (1974), 1250.

Pandey, R.E. "Factor Analytic Study of Attitudes Toward Death among College Students." *International Journal of Social Psychiatry* 21 (1974-75), 7-11.

Spielberger, C.D., R.L. Gorsuch, and R.E. Lushene. *STAI Manual for the State-Trait Anxiety Inventory* ("Self-Evaluation Questionnaire.") California: Consulting Psychologists Press, 1970.

Templer, D.I. "The Construction and Validation of a Death Anxiety Scale." *Journal of General Psychology* 82 (1970), 165-77.

--- and E. Dotson. "Religious Correlates of Death Anxiety." *Psychological Reports* 26 (1970), 895-97.

---, C.F. Ruff, and C.M. Franks. "Death Anxiety: Age, Sex, and Parental Resemblance in Diverse Populations." *Developmental Psychology* 4 (1971), 108.

--- and C.F. Ruff. "Death Anxiety Scale Means, Standard Deviation and Embedding." *Psychological Reports* 29 (1971), 173-74.

Wilcox, S.G. and M. Sutton. *Understanding Death and Dying: An Interdisciplinary Approach*, pp. 7-9. New York: Alfred A. Knopf, 1977.

10

Talking with Children About Death – Six Pragmatic Guides

Stanley D. Savicki

The death of a significant person in their immediate life
context has an immeasurable impact on children. Often,
children lack preparation for such an event because no one
has broached the topic of death with them until the crisis
situation occurs. The manner in which death is discussed per-
vasively affects not only the present emotional status but
also the subsequent development of the child. Because of
various factors, the discussion of death often proves difficult
for children and adults alike, with all feeling uneasy and
distressed. The tendency to avoid the topic of death is easily
accommodated but should be actively prevented. Children need
to explore the meaning of death openly and directly as an
essential element for their well-being and emotional growth
(Grollman 1967, 1974, 1976).

Six clear and concise guides are offered in this chapter
to help maximize the effectiveness of talking with children
about death. They should prove to be beneficial for both
children and adults during this important moment of meaningful
family interaction.

CHILDREN'S AWARENESS

Even those common parts of normal daily living--movies,
television, books, magazines, childhood stories, rhymes and
games--contain allusions to and facts about death. Even a
brief reflection will bring to mind examples of this pervasiveness and show how relatively difficult (and purposeless) it is
to shield children from the concept of death. Concerned
adults cannot prevent this exposure; rather, they can hope to
be able to direct children's inevitable thoughts and feelings
about death in a realistic and nonthreatening direction.

Children at various ages possess distinctively different concepts of death (Schowalter et al. 1983; Gullo et al. 1985). Around the age of three to four they generally lack a clear understanding of the nature of death. For them, there is no clearcut separation between "being alive" and "being dead." Death is simply a temporary departure, with the deceased continuing to eat, sleep, and breathe as people are normally expected to do.

This failure to differentiate between life processes and death gradually changes and by the age of five, the child begins to make a definite distinction. Between the ages of five and nine, children begin to have a more realistic concept of death. They begin to accept its pervasiveness and definitiveness. It is very common for children of these ages to personify death and consider it a unique entity or person: a skeleton, a ghost, a spook, and so forth. Ideas of personal death, on the other hand, are held remote and not inevitable.

After the age of nine, death becomes recognized as the total and irreversible termination of biological life. These more rational themes of the inevitability and irreversibility of death closely correspond to adult concepts and contain emerging thoughts about an afterlife.

PREVENTING CONFUSION, ISOLATION, AND INSECURITY

Children's concepts about death are often cluttered with unrealistic imaginings, misconceptions, fantasies, and confusion. When a child is faced with death for the first time, the direct and immediate intervention of a concerned adult can help clarify misconceptions, prevent isolation, and instill a sense of security in the child.

This important task can be accomplished by involving the child in family events and avoiding removal of the child from the family setting during the funeral period. Constant engagement of the child in activities and soliciting his or her views and opinions whenever possible are constructive, as is reinforcing, directly and indirectly, the child's importance as a person. Having someone available to answer children's questions and listen to their fears, apprehensions, thoughts, and ideas about death and the deceased intensifies the sense of family security and belonging.

WHO SHOULD TALK WITH THE CHILD?

The ideal person to talk with the child about death is anyone whom the child can trust, have confidence in, and feel is both open and sincere. These characteristics are essential and are as important as the actual content of the discussion itself. In response to these qualifications, the child feels free to express innermost thoughts, fears, and concepts about what is happening.

The initial uneasiness and reluctance of adults to confront the phenomenon of death with a child for the first time can easily be overcome. First, the adult should admit that death is a great mystery and that no single person can know all the answers about it. Second, the adult should realize that silence about death does not eliminate its impact but only exaggerates it. Third, the adult should appreciate that the real benefits of an open discussion derive from its content as well as from the emotional interaction with a person who really cares.

WHAT TO SAY

While each person must in his own way handle this issue by taking into account the age, mental development, and sensitivities of the child, there are several aids that help to initiate open confrontation and foster its continuance. Once a private area for an undisturbed person-to-person conversation is found, an assimilation of the past, present, and future in relation to the deceased and the child should begin. A helpful starting point is a review of the meaning that the deceased has had for the involved adult and the child in the past. "What do you remember most about . . . ?" "Do you remember when . . . ?" "What did you like most about . . . ?" "If you could tell . . . one more thing, what would you say?"

Talking about the future should stress the permanence of death and how the absence of the deceased will affect ongoing lives. Along with these ideas a sense of security and stability should be instilled: "Things will be different now, but we'll always remember the many good times together." "We're really going to miss . . . . What will you miss the most?"

All conversations should instill an honest understanding of death. Children usually have very simple questions requiring very simple and pragmatic answers: "Where do you go when you die?" "Why do people die?" "Do you still eat and breathe when you're dead?" Overanswering the child's inquiry with mystifying philosophical interpretations and statements that only add to the confusion should be avoided. The questions should be answered as they come: directly, briefly, truthfully. Open discussion is thus facilitated and the use of falsehoods, which only must be unlearned later, is avoided. There is no need to hesitate using the words "die" and "dead." These are very familiar to our media oriented youth. The child's concerns should be explored and the

realistic should be separated from the unrealistic. The
child can "lead" the direction of the conversation and guide
the adult's responses by his statements and questions.
This can be facilitated by a nondirective approach of asking
the child questions about areas he has shown interest in,
followed by the rephrasing and organizing of his comments.
This permits the continuation of the discussion, shows that
the adult really understands, and helps clarify the child's
own thoughts and ideas.

CHILDREN AND FUNERALS

It appears that children who are old enough to understand and be aware of surrounding events are old enough to be
given the opportunity to participate at a funeral. While
many children may not totally understand the mourning rituals,
a sense of security and order is generally derived from
simply being present at an important family event (Jackson
1957). However, the choice of attending or not attending
should rest with the individual. A child who prefers not to
attend, is overly sensitive, or who would fail to derive a
beneficial and meaningful experience because of the prevail-
ing circumstances should not be involved. Instead, other
family activities can be substituted as alternatives.
For most children who desire to participate, a few
simple guides can complement the experience. Before the
funeral, the child should be told what to expect and what
will occur. This advance explanation will minimize potential
confusion and prepare the child. During the funeral period,
the needs and questions of the child should be responded
to. Subsequent to the funeral, active solicitation and conversation about death and the deceased should be pursued
to clarify misconceptions and explore the event's meaning and
impact on the child (Grollman 1974).
Members of the funeral service profession can be supportive by being familiar with information concerning children
and death and by providing interested individuals with useful
resource material. They can also suggest an opportunity for
children to visit the funeral home with their family prior
to the public ceremony. This allows family confrontation in
a personal, caring, and uninterrupted fashion. Provisions for
an area exclusively for children where they can "get away,"
read, or talk among themselves, during the public visitation,
may also prove helpful.

BENEFITS OF AN OPEN APPROACH

The successful handling of this crisis in the life of the
child has enormous consequences. As a result, the child

becomes more realistically aware of life's total environment (of which death is a part); family solidarity is intensified with particular attention to a strengthened parent-child relationship; maladaptive fears, anxiety, and misconceptions are circumvented; and the child emerges with an increased sense of self-esteem, worth, importance, and security.

The caring adult also reaps a benefit. In addition to knowing that a child had been helped, through the process the adult, in some way, comes a little closer to acceptance of death as part of the life cycle (Feifel 1959; Fulton 1965; Toynbee 1969).

REFERENCES

Feifel, H., ed. *The Meaning of Death*. New York: McGraw-Hill, 1959.

Fulton, R. *Death and Identity*. New York: John Wiley, 1965.

Grollman, E.A., ed. *Explaining Death to Children*. Boston: Beacon Press, 1967.

---. *Concerning Death: A Practical Guide for the Living*. Boston: Beacon Press, 1974.

---. *Talking About Death--A Dialogue Between Parent and Child*. Boston: Beacon Press, 1976.

Gullo, S.V., P.R. Patterson, J.E. Schowalter, M. Tallmer, A.H. Kutscher, and P. Buschman, eds. *Death and Children: A Guide for Educators, Parents and Caregivers*. Dobbs Ferry, N.Y.: Tappan Press, 1985.

Jackson, E.N. *Understanding Grief--Its Roots, Dynamics, and Treatment*. New York: Abingdon Press, 1957.

Kutscher, A.H. and L.G. Kutscher, eds. *Religion and Bereavement*. New York: Health Sciences Publishing, 1972.

Schowalter, J.E., P.R. Patterson, M. Tallmer, A.H. Kutscher, S.V. Gullo, and D. Peretz, eds. *The Child and Death*. New York: Columbia University Press, 1983.

Toynbee, A. *Man's Concern with Death*. New York: McGraw-Hill, 1969.

11

Son's Reaction
to Father's Death
Resulting in Psychosis

Tamara Ferguson
and
Garfield Tourney

The literature on children who have lost a parent indicates that very young children cannot understand the concept of death, whereas older children may deny the reality of the death and fantasize about the lost parent (Mitchell 1967; Anthony 1972). The emotional reactions of children have been described, and it has been suggested that adolescents who lose a father experience reactivation of the Oedipus complex as they identify with the lost father and try to replace him. Furthermore, mothers compound this problem by projecting some of the expectations they had of their husband onto their son (Furman 1970; Furman 1974; Birtchnell 1969). This paper examines the reactions of young men to the loss of their fathers and, in particular, the psychotic reactions of four hospitalized patients. These reactions are discussed within the framework of a biopsychosocial theory of interaction--rescaling theory--which allows differentiation between schizophrenic and manic depressive patients. This theory may provide a partial explanation for the extreme behavior of some psychotic adolescents who have lost their fathers and, along with the usual treatment methods for psychoses, may assist in the treatment of such patients.

RESCALING THEORY

Rescaling theory is concerned with the balance between expectations and performance. Each person has both self and other expectations. By self-expectations, we mean what a person wants for himself and will do for others; by other-expectations we mean what one believes the other person will do for him and wants for himself. Ideally, expectations between two persons would be complementary, but in reality a person's self expectations and performance rarely match perfectly with his expectations of others and their performance. We suggest that expectations are defined in a series of life vectors, or physiological, psychological, and social potentials for development. There are 16 life vectors: shelter, food, health, motor development, speech, social life, art, politics, education, sex, occupation, finance, parenthood, ethics, law, and religion. A person's total vector balance is the balance between his self-expectations and performance and his expectations of others and their performance in the 16 life vectors.

We propose that imbalance between expectations and performance creates stress. When faced by an imbalance in a life vector, a person can use effective or ineffective means of regaining balance. When rescaling, he modifies expectations and performance and/or negotiates with the other person so that they both adjust their behavior. It is a conscious and effective way for a person to deal with his imbalance and with the consequent stress he experiences. However, a person may not be able to achieve a realistic appraisal of his problems because of his defense mechanisms and, in an effort to alleviate his stress, he may react automatically by using one or several of the following patterns of reactions:

Brutalization: the subject physically or verbally forces his performance on another person.

Victimization: the subject submits to the performance of another even though this negates his self and other expectations.

Self-brutalization: the subject physically or verbally forces a performance upon himself.

Insulation: the subject refuses to perform either by withdrawing physically or by refusing to talk about certain topics.

These patterns of reaction are ineffective in that they do not reduce a person's imbalance and stress. Indeed, these patterns may even compound imbalance because the person may start worrying about his reaction pattern.

INTERACTION BETWEEN WIDOWS AND THEIR SONS

A survey of 100 widows done in 1964-65 at the Bureau of Applied Social Research, Columbia University, showed the wide range of problems experienced by widows in most of their life vectors (Ferguson 1969, 1973). Old family roles such as looking after their husbands were taken from them, while new responsibilities such as earning a living were thrust upon them. Severe emotional, as well as psychosomatic reactions to their loss made it difficult for them to decide on a new life style, especially because in most marriages the husband was the person with whom the women discussed their problems.

The adolescent sons of the widows found themselves in a precarious position because loss of their fathers occurred at a period in their lives when they were trying to determine what their life expectations should be, and when they were not sure whether their own performances and the performances of others would match. For example, one young man found himself in financial difficulties. Instead of going to the college of his choice, he had to quit school, earn a living, help his mother to move to a smaller house, do her house repairs, give her advice, keep her company, and look after his siblings. Thus, he became engrossed in the welfare of his family instead of being able to move into the larger society to which he aspired. Mother and son were in an ambiguous situation because they both had to devise new expectations and performances and because their interests were often at cross purposes.

The findings of the survey showed that the adjustment that the widows made depended, to a certain extent, on the type of marital interaction they had with their husbands. Marital interaction was analyzed in terms of decision-making and whether there was high or low marital conflict between husband and wife in each of five roles: occupational, financial, social life, sexual, and parental. Basically, dominant widows with low marital conflict did not sufficiently take into consideration that their situation had changed and tended to be single-minded about the resolution of their problems. Dependent widows with low marital conflict relied too much on the advice of other people. Fifty-four of the widows had sons between ten and twenty years old. We found that 75 percent of the widows with high marital conflict ($N = 8$), as compared to only 7 percent of the widows with low marital conflict ($N = 46$), reported severe disciplinary problems with their sons. On the other hand, 25 percent of the widows with low marital conflict were concerned that they had become "too close" to their sons, whereas only one of the widows with high marital conflict expressed this concern.

The widows displaced some of the expectations they had of their husbands onto their sons. Because of that, dominant widows with high marital conflict tended to believe that their self-expectations were more important than their sons' expectations, and thus brutalized the sons. Dependent widows with low marital conflict tended to consider their sons' expectations more important than their own and allowed themselves to be victimized. Some widows alternated between these patterns of reactions. These widows felt sorry for their sons because they had lost their fathers, and therefore

overindulged them. Then they became annoyed at their sons'
lack of maturity and punished them. Sons who identified with
their fathers were torn between a desire to emulate their
fathers and protect their mothers and their longing to make
a life for themselves. By trying unconsciously to make their
sons replace their fathers, the widows were denying their
husbands' deaths and their sons were denying the loss of
their fathers.

SONS WHO DEVELOPED A PSYCHOSIS
REQUIRING HOSPITALIZATION

Both widows and their sons found it difficult to dis-
criminate between their self and other expectations. It
appears that the adolescents who were uncertain about this
distinction before their fathers died found it all the more
difficult to make it afterwards:

*Paul's father was a successful executive who
reacted to frustration by brutalizing others, by
getting drunk, and taking drugs, and by withdrawing. His mother emphasized that her son should
excel at school and brutalized him by taking out
the locks of his room so that she could check on
his behavior. She also was an alcoholic. Paul's
parents did not discuss with him what he should do
later on in life and did not give him any sexual
information. Paul's mother told him that she had a
lover and that this was a secret they shared. Paul
felt victimized because this information made his
relationship with his father more difficult to
handle.*

*When Paul was 13, his father died of a heart
attack. His mother had several boyfriends and
Paul said that he became very jealous of his
mother's lovers. Because of this, he brutalized
her by smashing phonograph records and breaking
some of the furniture. He was sent, against his
will, to a military school.*

*After Paul's graduation from high school, his
mother did not want him to live at home. He took
an apartment and enrolled in a college although he
was undecided about a career. He had high expectations and was aiming at an A average, but because
he was afraid that his performance would not match
his expectations, he did not attend school regu-
larly or take examinations. His aunt, who wanted
him to succeed, went to class and took notes for
him. She also brought him frozen food that he dis-*

liked, but felt he could not refuse to accept.
Paul fell in love with a girl he saw at a party,
but never dared to talk to her. Brutalizing
himself, he started to take drugs, became more
and more involved in the drug scene, had a car
accident, and was arrested. Later on, when hospi-
talized, he believed that the Mafia was after him.

Paul was diagnosed as schizophrenic, paranoid type. He was given Haldol and, later on, Stelazine to control his anxiety and thinking disturbance. After a few weeks, through psychotherapy, he gained insight that his delusions and hallucinations were part of his illness. He was then discharged and sent to his home. Medication was prescribed and his follow-up care was to include also group psychotherapy. However, he went back to live with his mother, stopped taking his medicine, and dropped out of group therapy.

When Paul became psychotic and was hospitalized, he was living from one expectation to another and had stopped performing. He said he did not have "the courage" to make a sexual relationship with a woman because he believed that he would not be able to satisfy her sexually and socially. His mother had treated him as a confidant when she told him about her lover, and then he felt that she had betrayed him. His identification with his father may have increased his fear that he would be rejected by his mother--and that like him, he would die and "disappear." Learning had also been presented to him as an invasion of his privacy, a brutalization, with his mother taking the lock off his room and his aunt taking notes for him.

Thus, it appears that Paul had never learned to distinguish between his self-expectations and his other-expectations, and that his interactions with others were unpredictable as he switched from one pattern of reaction to another as his father had done: he brutalized his mother by breaking her furniture, but he let himself be victimized by eating his aunt's frozen dinners and allowing her to take notes for him. Furthermore, he brutalized himself by taking drugs and he insulated himself first by refusing to talk to the woman he loved and later by dropping out of group therapy. His delusion of being persecuted by the Mafia may have been a symbolic representation of the degradation to which he had been subjected and had submitted himself. His failure to continue the pharmacology and group psychotherapy probably led to subsequent psychotic decompensation.

Another patient, Bob, was diagnosed as schizophrenic, schizoaffective type. Before his father's death, Bob was able to function, but only in a small number of life vectors defined by his mother.

Bob was his mother's confidant and her youngest child. They both worried because his father, who owned a store, had high blood pressure, a violent temper, and was in debt. Bob worked six days a week cutting lawns, trying to help his father financially.

Bob had a lonely youth. His mother did not allow him to go out in the evening because "she worried about him." He would have liked to get married eventually and have children, but "had never kissed a girl because he did not know how to kiss." His parents encouraged him to have children but discouraged him from getting married. Bob said that his mother was "nice but made you feel you should do things differently."

When Bob was 19, his father went to a party and died of a heart attack. Bob felt very guilty that he had allowed his father to go to the party. He became psychotic, and one day ran into the street, stopping cars with an empty pellet gun and asking the motorists, "Where is my father?"

When hospitalized, Bob alternated between being depressed and having fits of anger. He was given lithium and thorazine and, after a few weeks of psychotherapy, gained the insight that his delusion had been part of his illness. Bob would have liked to become a gardener, but felt that he should help his mother move to a smaller house and get a job "to help her to pay the bills." When he was discharged, he was able to hold a menial job and went on seeing a therapist.

Both Paul and Bob had been mystified by their mothers (Laing 1967). Some of their self-expectations had been imposed on them by their mothers, but they were really powerless to carry them out: Paul could not prevent his father from learning that his wife had a lover; Bob could not train his father to become a successful businessman. His parents, by suggesting to Bob that he should have children but not get married, mystified him even more.

Manic depressive adolescents appeared to find it difficult to decide whether their self-expectations were more important than their other-expectations, and thus switched back and forth between imposing their behavior on others and feeling guilty for their deeds.

John was 13 years old when his father, whom he had nursed for two years, died of cancer. Four years later, John was arrested by the police while driving away with a delivery van. He was incoherent when arrested and was sent to a mental hospital. When interviewed, he said that he had been obsessed by

*his father's death and had heard recurring songs
that "he should color his father" and that his
father was pleading with him that "he should keep
the family together." At first, John had violent
episodes, tearing the bulletin board and telling
other patients that they should not take their
medication because it was poisoned. Afterward,
he would have fits of depression.*

*John calmed down after he was able to cry and
express his grief at his father's death. It also
helped when it was pointed out to him that he did
not have to imitate his father, and like him,
react to frustration with anger followed by depression. John was also very distressed that his
girlfriend was dating someone else. His parents
believed that premarital sex was sinful and John
had learned the facts of life "in the street." He
was a virgin and was very preoccupied that he had
a strong sex drive. A collage hat he had made
showed the stern face of Nixon, a father figure,
in the middle of pinup girls. John felt that he
should look after his mother and younger siblings,
and his unresolved Oedipus complex was evident
when he called his nephew his grandson. He was not
sure whether he should join the Navy or go back to
school.*

John was first diagnosed as being schizophrenic and given
Haldol, which yielded a minimal change in his condition. A
diagnosis of manic depressive was then considered and he
was given lithium with favorable clinical results. This was
believed to support the diagnosis of manic depression. His
main conflict appeared to be that he alternated between
believing that he should obey his father's admonition to keep
the family together and the feeling that what mattered to
him was to win back his girlfriend's love.

When interviewed six months after discharge, John was
studying in a community college. His occupational plans were
still vague. He had put on 20 pounds, and said that his sex
drive was much less strong and that he was calmer. He felt
that his best decision was to accept the fact that he should
take lithium for the rest of his life. He was still a virgin
and was going out with his former girlfriend and her new
boyfriend. When he was asked why he did not have a girlfriend
of his own, he said "there must be something wrong with my
blood." He was doubtful that he should marry and have children. He was also afraid that he might have another break-
down if he worked while going to school. He was financially
dependent on his mother, who had recently given up her part-
time job.

John said that what had helped him most during his hospitalization was that in work and group therapy he had learned
to select a job, do it well, and finish it, and that this
experience had helped him to get a summer job. In other
words, he had learned to achieve a balance between expectations
and performance, at least in one life vector.

The manic depressive adolescent with primarily depression
was rarely satisfied with his performance.

> *Ed was eight when his father, a skilled worker,
> died. His father was a man who reacted to frustra-
> tion with anger. After his father's death, Ed
> started commuting between his mother and grand-
> parents, who were very critical of each other. He
> lived with his grandparents but took his meals with
> his mother, and was not happy with this arrangement.
> He was broken-hearted when his grandfather died.*
>
> *Ed felt that his mother "was running his life
> because she had no husband." She bought his clothes,
> cooked for him, and did not allow him to do any
> housework. He wanted to be an engineer, but when he
> first started to study he could not concentrate on
> his studies because he had fallen in love with a
> girl "but did not dare to approach her." He became
> depressed, was hospitalized, and only then learned
> the facts of life. For several years, he alternated
> between working and studying and periods of hos-
> pitalization.*
>
> *When interviewed, he was not sure whether he
> would complete his studies. He would have liked
> to get married and have children "to give them what
> he did not have and be somebody."*

Ed had been treated with many drugs, and eventually responded
well to antidepressant medication. It appears that, like his
father, he became angry when frustrated and then, like his
mother, became depressed and withdrew. Perhaps becoming an
engineer would have required that he give up behaving as his
mother's substitute husband.

DISCUSSION

The four psychotic adolescents discussed above have in
common the death of their fathers and the employment of various
defense mechanisms in order to cope with their loss over a
prolonged time. Study of these four patients reveals that
bereavement can be seen as a significant precipitant for the
development of psychosis. This period of bereavement may
evolve over a period of several years, during which the mother's

problems with widowhood and transference of her difficulties
with her husband may in some way reflect on the son. The
sons do not develop any specific psychosis as a result of
these circumstances—both schizophrenic and manic depressive
illness have been seen.

With psychotic sons, the standard therapeutic measures
are used, including psychopharmacologic agents and psychotherapy. We raise the question of the mother's need for
special treatment of her own behavior process because her
attempts at resolution involve her son with disastrous consequences. In these four cases, no therapy of the mothers as
such was carried out. This may have impaired the results and
had adverse effects, particularly on their schizophrenic
sons.

It appears that it is easier to identify the defense
mechanisms of bereaved psychotic adolescents than to identify
those of adolescents who have not been bereaved in their
identification with their father. When their father is dead,
the son cannot check the accuracy of his expectations by
comparing them with his father's performance. Thus, he has
an idealized image of his father and, perhaps because of
this, he has unbounded expectations. His mother, by displacing some of her expectations of her husband onto her son,
makes it more difficult for him to assert himself.

The schizophrenic patient appears the most confused:
he does not know the boundaries between his ill-defined self-
and other-expectations. His defense mechanisms distort his
expectations and, by randomly using different patterns of
reactions to deal with the stress he experiences, he compounds
his alienation. His total vector balance is very low because
he cannot match his conflicting and fluctuating expectations
through his performance.

The manic depressive alternates between trying to achieve
high, even grandiose, self-expectations and equally high
other-expectations. He rarely realizes his self-expectations
because they are too high. Then he becomes depressed and
tries to fulfill the other-expectations. He fails again
because his expectations are again too high, and he becomes
angry that he has allowed himself to be victimized. Of course,
this partial explanation of the dynamics of schizophrenia and
manic depressive illness is tentative. The genetic predis-
position of the patient and the biochemical changes that may
occur under stress cannot be ignored. The theory needs further
testing, but the findings of an exploratory survey of 40 in-
patients give preliminary support to this explanation.

Most psychological testing procedures have been used as
diagnostic instruments. However, the main purpose of rescaling theory is to locate the different areas of behavior and
the time period when the patient becomes unable to distinguish
between his self and other expectations or starts to experi-

ence a conflict of expectations. The study of the patient's defense mechanisms provides us with an explanation of why he cannot assess a situation realistically and may hold on to some obsolete expectations. Patterns of reactions describe his actual performance and the manner in which he further alienates himself from others.

The theory also specifies the power relationships in the primary group, making it clear who is brutalizing whom and revealing the different patterns of reaction family members use to mystify each other (Lidz and Fleck 1960; Laing 1969). Thus the theory allows us to focus quickly on the main social problems of the patient and to explain them to him theoretically, cast in readily intelligible terms of everyday interaction. This approach may be useful with adolescent sons who have lost their fathers because a realistic assessment of their new goals is important to their social functioning.

REFERENCES

Anthony, S. *The Discovery of Death in Childhood and After*. New York: Basic Books, 1972.

Birtchnell, J. "The Possible Consequences of Early Parent Death." *British Journal of Medical Psychology* 42 (1969), 1-12.

Ferguson, T. "Decision Making and Tranquilizers in Widowhood." In I.K. Goldberg, S. Malitz, and A.H. Kutscher, eds., *Psychoparmacologic Agents for the Terminally Ill and Bereaved*, pp. 225-34. New York: Columbia University Press, 1973.

---. "How Young Widows Have Coped with Their Problems." In A.H. Kutscher, ed., *But Not To Lose*, pp. 198-214. New York: Frederick Fell, 1969.

Furman, E. "The Child's Reaction to Death in the Family." In B. Schoenberg et al., eds., *Loss and Grief: Psychological Management in Medical Practice*, pp. 70-86. New York: Columbia University Press, 1970.

---. *A Child's Parent Dies*. New Haven: Yale University Press, 1974.

Laing, R.D. "The Politics of Experience." In *The Politics of Experience and the Bird of Paradise*. London: Penguin Books, 1969.

Lidz, T. and S. Fleck. "Schizophrenia, Human Interaction and the Role of the Family." In D.D. Jackson, ed., *The*

Etiology of Schizophrenia, pp. 323-45. New York: Basic Books, 1960.

Mitchell, M.E. *The Child's Attitude to Death*. New York: Schocken Small Books, 1967.

12

The Elderly, Death, and Bereavement Planning

Virginia W. Barrett

Thanatology and gerontology have a great deal in common in that both are new fields concerned with old realities. The stages observable in dying and bereavement are similar to those seen in aging, and both processes are characterized by depletion, isolation, loss, illness, and finality. The pressures of a limited lifespan are the same in both situations, requiring changes in allocation of time, effort, and resources (Kalish 1976). In addition, psychological and social disengagement is a characteristic response to the anticipation of death present in both of these situations (Weisman 1972). The aging individual, however, has more frequent and continual reminders of approaching death: decline of mental and physical function, reduced recuperative ability, cohort deaths, and social disenfranchisement by the society. Does this mean that it is easier for the old to die? Do the elderly feel that longevity is really long enough?

The literature on the terminal elderly is limited, fragmented, contradictory, and biased (Weisman 1972). Nevertheless, it is imperative that age-specific information be available to the professional staff in any setting where the work involves caring for elderly people who are terminally ill and bereaved (Herr and Weakland 1979). To meet the needs of this age group, we need to know more about who they are, what they die of, how they grieve, and finally, in what way this information can be used by the health care professionals who establish policies and who are involved in planning and carrying out procedures (Prichard et al. 1984).

In 1980, the more than 20 million people over the age of 65 in the United States constituted about 10 percent of the total population. By the year 2000, this age group will increase to between 16 and 20 percent and by 2015 will begin to approach 40 percent of the total population of the country.

In this age group, there are about 72 males to every 100 females. Among those between the ages of 64 and 74, 41 percent of the females and 9.3 percent of the males are widowed; among those over 75, these percentages rise to 69.7 percent and 24.3 percent, respectively (McKenzie 1980). In the mid-1970s, deaths of those over 65 constituted 70 percent of all deaths in the country. The primary causes of death in this age group are cardiovascular disease, cancer, and respiratory disease.

There are other facts that are helpful to consider when planning for care of the elderly. Within this group, 14.1 percent live on incomes that are below the poverty line (McKenzie 1980). Over 90 percent of the elderly reside in the community, 4 percent permanently reside in nursing homes, and 20 percent spend some period of time in a nursing home (Kalish 1976; McKenzie 1980). Members of this age group have the highest incidence of multiple chronic diseases. They also experience major losses, such as the loss of spouse, cohorts, employment, income, housing, health, and social status, with greater frequency than those in other age groups.

Professionals in the health fields respond differently to the elderly, and in many ways their responses reflect the prejudices of our society. As noted by Weisman (1972), little is expected from the elderly and little is offered to them. Health care professionals often minimize the complaints of the elderly and attribute to "old age" symptoms that cannot be eradicated (Weisman 1972). Professional staff spend less time in the emergency room pronouncing an older person dead (Kalish 1976). The elderly are not treated with the same care and concern that is shown when a younger patient is diagnosed as having a life-threatening disease (Weisman 1972). Moreover, we use expressions such as "his time had come" to illustrate our feeling that death is appropriate in old age. Such behaviors convey a disturbing message to the elderly patient and promote feelings of diminished social worth (Kalish 1976).

In one study it was found that the elderly, if aware of a specific time period to live, would make fewer changes in their lives than younger people would and would assume more inner-directed activities. They feel less concern with causing grief to friends and relatives than do younger adults. Among the elderly there is a higher rate of belief in a sequential time plan to life and in a relationship between being morally good and living a long time. The elderly also more often desire to die at home, and tend to view all types of death as equally upsetting (Prichard et al. 1979). It has also been concluded that the elderly patient may appear to be more ready to die, but not tomorrow (Kalish 1976).

Research on death anxiety and aging indicates a possibility that there is more denial of death among those most

threatened by it, as shown by the elderly's low overt anxiety
levels and high nonconscious anxiety levels (Schulz 1978), as
well as by their higher preference for a protective approach
in terminal care (Kalish 1976). In a 1971 study by Preston
and Williams, given the situation of fatal illness, great
distress, and heavy medical expenses, half of those elderly
surveyed favored being kept alive at all costs (Kalish 1976).

Grief reaction in the elderly is an area of gerontologi-
cal research in need of more attention, especially considering
the disproportionate and steadily increasing number of deaths
in this age group, the lack of third-party coverage to meet
care expenses during the bereavement period, and the fact that
when the elderly are not in a hospital, their needs are
invisible. The grief pattern of the elderly is atypical of
the accepted standard description of grief response in adults
(Gramlich 1974), a fact that needs to be considered when
making referrals, planning for community outreach, and
establishing bereavement counseling programs (Sinick 1977).

The few existing studies on this topic are frequently
contradictory, and suggest that in our youth-oriented society,
we are seeking answers by asking the wrong questions. What
is agreed on in the literature is that grief, which is often
overlooked as a potential cause of disease in the elderly, can
aggravate pre-existing disorders, and produce organic and
physiologic changes that may be confused with other conditions
of normal aging (Gramlich 1974). In this age group, the
grieving process often is not experienced on a conscious
level, but may be expressed through somatic complaints such
as gastrointestinal symptoms and joint and muscle pain
(Schulz 1978).

Because most early studies on bereavement were based on
surveys of younger adults, some conclusions have been reached
that may not apply to the elderly. An example of this is
the assumption that sudden death causes a more difficult
adjustment for survivors, whereas recent studies imply that
this reaction may be reversed in the elderly. Specific to
advanced age, an elderly survivor may feel guilt and resent-
ment if he or she expected, or was expected by others, to die
first. There is also a conflict between the need to express
feelings and the social constraints that make high demands
on the elderly to maintain composure. Finally, if an elderly
person's recovery from grief after the death of a spouse is
rapid and successful, making that person stronger and more
socially aggressive, family and friends who romanticize unsuccessful grieving as the appropriate response to the end of
many years of marriage may express disappointment.

Although the elderly do experience many of the grief
phases normally observed, they are at high risk of becoming
socially isolated if their prior life has not provided for
autonomy. It should also be recalled that the suicide rate

is higher among older males than any other segment of the population, and that suicides among the elderly constitute 25 percent of all reported suicides (Grollman 1974). These suicides are often related to unsuccessful grieving (Tallmer et al. 1984).

Addressing the role that community hospital professionals should assume in planning care for the terminal elderly, I shall first restate a question asked by Weisman, "In old age, everyone must rely upon others, even people like ourselves who are professionals. When this point arrives, what kind of people would you like to deal with?" (Weisman 1972, p. 157). In answer to this question, we should specify that in addition to other attributes, these people should be informed about age-specific needs, so that unique approaches might be explored in response to the unique problems of the elderly.

Planning for the elderly is planning for individuals who have had many years of making their own decisions. Therefore, caregivers must be collaborative as well as supportive. In bereavement planning, patients, families, professionals all need to believe in the ability of the elderly to cope with crisis. The greatest tragedy for people in this age group is that they themselves accept the stereotypes of mental and physical fragility, dependence, and obsolescence that we have imposed upon them.

Studies have shown that the elderly do not seek help in bereavement as frequently as do younger people. Therefore, the community hospital, as the primary point of entry into the health care system, has a responsibility not to limit its role to care of isolated individuals, but to reach out to their families as well. Hospital policies and staff attitudes that are paternalistic and make family members feel that their presence is inconvenient and intrusive need to be re-examined.

In the hospital, continuing education curriculum for all staff involved directly in patient care needs to include courses on subjects of terminal care and aging that are sup-portive as well as informative, and should include some vehicle for the re-examination of practices and attitudes (Marshall 1981). Continuing education courses should also concentrate on the communication skills needed in history-taking and documentation. It would be beneficial if progress notes on the terminal elderly patients included what they lived for as well as what they died from (Weisman 1972). Records should also note a plan for survival as well as demise (Parkes 1972), the degree to which alternative plans are either unsatisfactory or appropriate, plans for medical and psychotherapeutic follow-up, and communications with churches, social agencies, friends, and relatives regarding the needs of those who will survive the patient. After death has occurred, the hospital record needs to reflect ongoing com-munication with the community and should include information

on the progress and problems of the survivors and the pre-
ventive measures taken and treatments offered for the survivors. In the community, a public health nurse, social worker,
counselor, or self-help group should record and communicate
their interventions to help the bereaved eradicate guilt
feelings, reject irrational thoughts, accept and work out
hostilities, pursue recovery and socialization, and seek medical care for somatic complaints (Gramlich 1974).

Along with undertaking better documentation and communication, we need to be better listeners. How people feel about
dying and the way in which the bereavement period is experienced is influenced by the expectations of the society whose
beliefs we reflect. We need to listen to what we are saying
and not saying, because our expectations may become a self-
fulfilling prophesy (Weisman 1972). Planning for care of the
bereaved elderly requires special attention to the recognition
of danger signals such as changes in cognitive abilities,
self-starvation, failure to take prescribed medications,
hazardous activities, and voluntary seclusion (Grollman 1974).
Perhaps the target audience of death education courses should
be the elderly. This could allow them to be aware of the
dying process, to understand and prepare for the grief process,
and to be informed in their decisions.

The availability within the community of bereavement
counseling specific to the elderly and their families has
proven to be a positive step, but one in which the community
hospital might be more active in case finding, referral, and
organization. In counseling the elderly, it has been observed
that the primary concerns they express include depression and
its manifestations, including suicide, difficulties in develop-
ing new roles and in social relationships, and problems in
adjusting to losses (Burnside 1978). In group work, the
benefits to the elderly include heightened self-esteem with
awareness of shared problems, group identification, increasingly realistic self-image, and adaptation to environmental
change, as well as an increase in social opportunities,
greater awareness of available resources, and the development
of problem-solving techniques. By pursuing group work and
other actions that reflect belief in the abilities and social
value of older people, the health care community can elevate
the elderly's perception of themselves and lead them to feel
that survival is really worth the effort.

REFERENCES

Burnside, I. *Working With the Elderly, Group Process and
     Techniques*. Massachusetts: Duxbury Press, 1978.

Gramlich, E. "Recognition and Management of Grief in Elderly
     Patients." In J. Ellard et al., eds., *Normal and Patho-*

logical Responses to Bereavement. New York: MSS Information Corporation, 1974.

Grollman, E. *Concerning Death: A Practical Guide for the Living.* Boston: Beacon Press, 1974.

Herr, J.J. and J.H. Weakland. *Counseling Elders and Their Families, Practical Techniques for Applied Gerontology,* pp. 287-96. New York: Springer, 1979.

Kalish, R. "Death and Dying in a Social Context." In R.H. Binstock and E. Shanas, *Handbook of Aging and the Social Sciences,* pp. 483-504. New York: Van Nostrand Reinhold, 1976.

Marshall, J.R. "The Dying Patient." In W. Reichel, ed., *Topics in Aging and Long Term Care,* pp. 223-27. Baltimore: Williams and Company, 1981.

McKenzie, S.C. *Aging and Old Age.* Illinois: Scott, Foresman and Company, 1980.

Parkes, C.M. *Bereavement: Studies of Grief in Adult Life.* London: Tavistock, 1972.

Prichard, E.R. et al., eds. *Home Care: Living with Dying.* New York: Columbia University Press, 1979.

---, M. Tallmer, A.H. Kutscher, R. DeBellis, and M.S. Hale, eds. *Geriatrics and Thanatology.* New York: Praeger, 1984.

Schulz, R. *The Psychology of Death, Dying, and Bereavement.* Reading, Mass.: Addison-Wesley, 1978.

Sinick, D. *Counseling Older Persons: Careers, Retirement, Dying,* pp. 57-77. New York: Human Sciences Press, 1977.

Tallmer, M., E.R. Prichard, A.H. Kutscher, R. DeBellis, M.S. Hale, and I.K. Goldberg, eds. *The Life-Threatened Elderly.* New York: Columbia University Press, 1984.

Weisman, A.D. *On Dying and Denying.* New York: Behavioral Publications, 1972.

Part IV

Guiding the Bereaved

13

Immediate and Extended Postdeath Activities

Howard C. Raether

As a professional on the American "dying, death, and
bereavement scene" for over 35 years, I know how insignificant
the contributions of one person dealing with "life *and* death"
might have been. However, I am also aware that one person
benefitting by the knowledge, thought processes, research
ability, and experiences of others can make a contribution.
It should be clearly understood that without the support of
the efforts of many funeral service practitioners, funeral
service educators, clergypersons, sociologists, psychologists,
a psychiatrist, and some experts in marketing and management,
the achievement of many of my personal goals could not have
been possible. These goals have involved the most important
challenges facing postdeath activities and confrontation with
major issues in postdeath activities.

The organizational leadership of funeral service practice
in the United States reflects developments that will affect
the future of postdeath activities in the United States and
proposes enlightened guidelines for a specific group of professionals who conduct their business with consumers who are
functioning during a period of heightened stress. The basic
format in the United States of licensing those who provide the
postdeath care of the deceased body and those who survive is
different from that in most other countries. Therefore,
encroachment by unlicensed purveyors who make available the
same services offered by those licensed as funeral directors
and/or embalmers, looms threateningly in the United States.
The reasons for these alleged encroachments and the diminution
of what was once deemed essential are important because human
nature is what it is. Just as much of what constitutes
American funeral customs originated outside of the United
States, certain trends in the United States could affect practices in other countries. Therefore, it is fitting to detail

some of the concerns of today's funeral service practitioners and their leaders.

The size of most families in many of the nations of the world is decreasing. There is also an increased mobility of members of the family depending on size, status, and income.

Undoubtedly, in many nations the family will continue to be extended, that is, there will be more than the parents and children of a family within a household. It is predicted that the nuclear family (parents and children in a household) will prevail in some nations, especially those which are highly industrialized.

In some cultures, there will be those who will want to maintain tradition and be involved in postdeath activities. However, within the past 50 years, some families have called on functionaries who were "service specialists" to do for them what they once did for themselves. There now is evidence of a trend back to having families doing at least *some* things for themselves following death even though a paid functionary may be involved to do other things (Pine et al. 1976; Margolis et al. 1981).

It is difficult, arbitrarily and generally, to assign any particular role to family members or to a functionary whom they may choose to call when a death occurs. It is easy, however, to suggest that, regardless of the situation, the family as a unit or as individuals within that unit be given as much information as possible prior to the time that a death occurs, including a predeath visit to a funeral establishment. That information should relate to immediate postdeath activities, rituals and the costs involved. This will eliminate some of the so-called mystique about death, and some of the negative attitudes toward postdeath activities. Ignorance about death and that which follows it is not bliss, nor is the state of bereavement, loss, and grief. But appropriately given advice and information can alleviate the shock of loss and prepare survivors for their grief work.

The age at which death occurs results in varying responses to that death. There are instances where the grief potential is very low. This is especially true where individuals have outlived their contemporaries and often the ability to provide for themselves. On the other hand, there are instances where the grief potential is very high. This is especially true where there is the death of the breadwinner of the family, a spouse, or that of a child.

When people are elderly or have been ill for a long time, they become separated from their community. Because they are out of sight, they are out of mind. And, when they are out of mind, they are out of heart. When they die, it is said that there are few who really care enough to want to participate in some sort of postdeath activities (Keith 1984).

Few welcome death, even though it may bring release and relief. However, the fact that certain deaths have a low grief potential as compared to others with a high grief potential cannot be refuted. Because individuals are domiciled in an extended care facility or a hospital or in a senior citizen area, it does not mean that they are removed from society to the point where postdeath activities have no meaning. The survivors in the community and the facility where death occurs want to grieve and it is proper to provide them with a vehicle to do so.

When an elderly parent dies, there are children who feel that there is nothing that should be done to acknowledge their death. Yet in many instances those adult children have children who are the grandchildren of the deceased. Or, their children have children who are the great-grandchildren of the deceased. The grandchildren and great-grandchildren often want to have some sort of ceremony for their grandparent or great-grandparent and they want to be there for it. There are those saying that some of the trends away from funeralization for elderly persons could develop into a very unhealthy situation. It could result in grandchildren or great-grandchildren not wanting to have children of their own because they witnessed what their parents or grandparents did to their parents and they would not want that to happen to them if they became parents.

Some problems for the bereaved are generated within the place where death occurs. Deaths occur at home, in hospitals, in extended care facilities or places of employment, or on the streets or highways. In the United States, where most deaths occur in medical institutions, families are isolated from the death scene. This sometimes encourages the denial of the death because the members of the family are not there when it occurs or shortly thereafter. When death comes after a lingering illness, family members' hospital visits are limited. A once-a-day visit soon becomes a visit once or twice a week. In the meantime, the medical facility personnel assume the role of surrogate family members. When death occurs they become surrogate grievers. These facts become important in making arrangements for postdeath activities when often the caregivers' attitudes toward the members of the immediate family become hostile.

There is nothing much that those involved in immediate postdeath activities can do to have members of families become more involved with their ill family member. However, medical personnel can be made aware of the value of postdeath activities. This awareness will lead to discussions between such caregivers and the members of the family so that when death does occur, the members of the family will be able to proceed with dignity and equanimity.

The hospice movement is not new when one takes a look at the world as such. It is a new phenomenon in the United

States. The foundation of the hospice, which is family care as well as participation in medical services as delivered by others, is a big step in the right direction. A hospice allows the family to become involved in immediate postdeath activities as once was done years ago (Kutscher et al. 1983).

In many parts of the world man's relationship to God has changed. While there are many people who believe in a divine being, there are fewer people whose belief is associated with a particular religion or religious denomination. In many religions and denominations the influence of the church is on the wane. However, it is still a powerful force. Those ordained within a particular religion have an influence over those who practice their religion and even those who might attend church only rarely. The fact is that most people do want a clergyperson to participate in the funeral.

In the United States, we have known for at least twenty years that the more education a person has, the greater his or her earning capacity will be; the greater this earning capacity, the less will be a person's religiosity; and, the less the religiosity, the greater the chances are for a negative approach toward any postdeath activities. The evidence is empirical. As a result, those who educate at all levels--grade school, middle school, high school and college --have a tendency, if not compulsion, to be critical of any rituals and ceremonies that follow death. Perhaps such educators are scared to death of death because of their own mortality, because of an ambivalent, if not negative, attitude toward religion. One of the reasons that persons with formal education have a negative view toward postdeath activities is that the education process, regardless of the level of education, has encouraged such views.

However, by presenting information on dying, death, and bereavement to those in schools, ranging from the fifth grade through college, it has been possible to change attitudes toward death and postdeath activities. It is strongly urged that whenever possible formalized courses be conducted so that fears can be erased and suspicions alleviated.

As annual cremation statistics are released, they probably will show a marked increase in the percentage of cremations to total deaths. What is happening to cause this acceleration in a practice that some 20 years ago was viewed as being nontraditional? Two reasons--cost and/or status symbol--bear examination.

Cremation avoids the cost of cemetery space and grave charges or mausoleum expense. It eliminates an outside receptacle into which the casketed body is placed--a receptacle required by many cemeteries to minimize maintenance costs. Furthermore, there are a growing number of people choosing cremation who select less expensive caskets. Finally, cremation eliminates the cost of a monument or marker and maintenance of the grave.

Cremation is also becoming a status symbol for some individuals. They like to feel that they are rising above tradition and taboo. The Episcopal Church in the United States is encouraging this trend by providing for the inurnment of cremated remains on the church grounds, if not as part of the church edifice. It might become significant if cremation became not a form of disposition of the body preceded by a rite or ceremony or as part of a ritual but all that there is to mark the death of a loved one. In fact, this is already happening when a functionary removes the body and shelters it until transporting it for final disposition after the necessary permits are obtained. This procedure is called "direct disposition."

Some years ago, some of us predicted that unless the value of postdeath activities was made clear, the role of the funeral director could be relegated to that of a transporter and disposer of dead human bodies. This admonition is valid for every country where there are functionaries who are paid for the services, facilities, and merchandise they offer to meet postdeath needs.

The postdeath customs of most cultures revolve around the body of the deceased. In the United States there is a segment of the population who believe the body should not be present for any rites, ceremonies, or memorialization. These people have organized "memorial societies." They currently indicate change from a funeral reform group to a consumer organization to provide facts and figures on all forms of postdeath activities. However, some of their leaders sincerely seek a postdeath rite that is nontraditional and nonreligious (without a body), if not a funeralless society.

Mourning practices have been changed or eliminated. In the United States black is no longer worn as *the* designation of mourning. Arm bands are fast disappearing. Door wreathes or ribbons may no longer announce a death in a particular household. Few people will stop what they are doing and stand in silence while a funeral cortege passes. Today we see persons who see no significance in personal responses to death, although some may permit some public responses without the body present.

While certain mourning practices might have been eliminated, mourning per se is not an outmoded custom. Although people have found ways of mourning that are not as comprehensive as they once were, they are not as meaningful. In many ways the "right to mourn" is a fact. There are labor unions whose members as part of their contract can attend the funeral of a near relative and get paid for the time taken off for such attendance. There are businesses that close on the day of a funeral of an associate. Even though there have been many moves made to eliminate the funeral procession by state law or county or municipal ordinance, none has been successful.

While there have been moves to restrict, if not eliminate mourning practices, the arguments against this happening carry

sufficient weight to mitigate against it. However, such
arguments will lose their validity if those who have opted
for mere disposition of the body with no rites or ceremonies
or just limited ones are able to intellectualize their
actions and separate completely human emotions from human
well-being.

Many feel that postdeath activities should be conducted
without the body present, even without any funeral or memorial service whatever. No one will argue that a living
person's body is sacred because it loves and is loved. However, some feel that when a body loses its life, it becomes
a profane object. Often for a dead body to be of benefit
to others it must be "medically acceptable" and "needed."
Many, of course, are not. Yet, is a dead body only something
"to get rid of"? Almost every culture since the beginning
of time has had postdeath ceremonies with the body present.
The presence of the body is essential to confirm the reality
of what has happened and, I believe, it is a *cohesive element*
for the various facets of postdeath activities.

Even in colonial America, there were laws and regulations to prohibit excessive funeral expenditures. These
prohibitions came from individuals who settled in the colo-
nies from Europe. The criticism of funeral expenditures has
been with us always and will continue to be. It becomes
necessary to show the economic and social utility of the
funeral. However, this can be done only by indicating that
everything should not be given a price tag. Generally,
criticism of postdeath expenditures comes from those who
have not had a death in their family. Their complaints are
stimulated by what is circulated in the media. Criticism
also comes from those who have had postdeath experiences and
want to exaggerate all aspects of these experiences to
relieve their own anxieties. Some individuals, unfortunately,
have had less than satisfactory funeral experiences.

The word "humankind" seems to have replaced "mankind."
Similarly, the services of the funeral functionary allow for
the dead to be cared for as a way of serving the living and
maintaining the dignity of humankind. In this chapter, I
have tried to look full circle at matters that confront those
who care for the dead and serve the living. Attitudes of
various cultures toward death and mourning are being reshaped.
Ritual must not be a passive reflector of cultural values.
It can participate in the structuring of these values. Postdeath activities can exert a potential influence upon the
thought and behavior of any culture. It can be a force in
stemming the flight from reality by affording the support
necessary to confront death and loss. Postdeath activities
can undergird acceptance and defiance of death rather than
denial of it. They can resist the separation of death from
life and enhance life's meaning by acknowledging the traumatic
encounter with the reality of death.

Thanatopractitioners no longer can restrict their activities to those of a predeath and immediate postdeath nature.
There must be an interest in extended postdeath activities.
There are concerned widows looking for adjustment assistance
and advice. There are parents about to be divorced because
of the death of an infant or young child. There are children
having difficulty facing life after the death of a parent or
sibling. All these people cry out for help. They seek a
place where they can get it and meet with others in the same
predicament as they are.

Is not this a role of the thanatopractitioner? Do not
these opportunities open doors where the living can be served
after the period of the funeral? Those involved daily with
death can be better catalysts to help identify those who need
help and provide some vehicles for giving it. Is not this an
extension of caregiving?

REFERENCES

Keith, R. "Death and the Elderly's Perception of Self-Worth."
In E.R. Prichard, M. Tallmer, A.H. Kutscher, R. DeBellis,
and M.S. Hale, eds., *Geriatrics and Thanatology*, pp. 161-
68. New York: Praeger, 1984.

Kutscher, A.H. S.C. Klagsbrun, R.J. Torpie, R. DeBellis, M.S.
Hale, and M. Tallmer, eds. *Hospice, U.S.A.* New York:
Columbia University Press, 1983.

Margolis, O.S., H.C. Raether, A.H. Kutscher, J.B. Powers, J.B.
Seeland, R. DeBellis, and D.J. Cherico, eds. *Acute
Grief: Counseling the Bereaved*. New York: Columbia
University Press, 1981.

Pine, V.R., A.H. Kutscher, D. Peretz, R.J. Slater, R. DeBellis,
R.J. Volk, and D.J. Cherico, eds. *Acute Grief and the
Funeral*. Springfield, Ill.: Charles C Thomas, 1976.

14

The Funeral Service Practitioner as a Counselor

Raoul L. Pinette

Many therapists question the value or the propriety of a funeral service practitioner serving as a counselor. It is the intent of this paper to show that not only is there an appropriate place in the large field of counseling for the funeral service practitioner but also that he fills a particular void that, unfortunately, still exists.

Because of new information developed in recent years, practitioners of academic disciplines such as psychiatry, psychology, sociology, social work, nursing, and others are better prepared to help those with special problems of grief. However, these professionals share a common problem! They must wait to be sought in order to become helpful. We know that they are not sought often enough and this is not subject to change rapidly.

When a death occurs, two practitioners are generally on location because they have been summoned: the clergyperson and the funeral director. There are many people today who have no religious commitment and no church affiliation; they would consider a religious service or the presence of the clergy to be hypocritical on their part and request that the clergy not be present at a funeral. The funeral director is the only one with whom the survivors have contact during the immediate postdeath crisis. The funeral director can, may, and must serve as a counselor.

When people come to him and ask for advice or information, the minute he responds he is counseling. The big question is not whether he is or is not a counselor. It is: "What is the quality of his counseling?" We are now talking about situational counseling. The funeral counselor does not have the preparation nor the desire to become involved in therapeutic counseling even though the funeral and related activities may have psychotherapeutic value for some.

The funeral counselor may also become involved in post-funeral counseling and this is where his intentions are questioned by some therapists who see him as an invader. It should be remembered that the counseling that the funeral counselor does is, and should be, on the basic level and should not be confused with therapy.

For those who are grieving the pain is severe, but most of these people do not consider themselves sick. For this they do not wish and will not consent to consult a therapist. They do not want to place themselves in a doctor-patient relationship.

The relationship that a grieving survivor has with the funeral counselor is a client relationship at certain times and at most times, even better still, a friend-to-friend relationship. Many bereaved persons find it easy to become involved in this kind of relationship. It does not generally appear to be counseling, but it is that and may be very effective.

The bereaved have certain basic needs:

1. They need a sympathetic ear, or better still, an empathetic ear to hear them, that is, a person who can listen well.

2. They need to talk to someone whom they feel understands them. As a funeral director who has experienced the death of his father, his mother, his wife, and two unborn children, I have authentic empathy to give to people in such situations. This cannot be replaced by sophisticated techniques, and it is received as genuine because my people know that I have worn the shoes.

3. They need someone to tell them that emotions are normal, that acute grief is normal, that many people have felt the way they now feel and that most people recover in time.

4. They seek answers and need to be told that no one has such answers, that they must resolve the situation for themselves in their own style.

5. They do need help, direction, guidance in organizing their thoughts. The funeral counselor can assist with conversation and by suggesting appropriate literature.

These are but a few examples of how the funeral service practitioner may, with simple and basic counseling, be very helpful to survivors. If he sees no signs of a resolution of the grief after approximately three months, I believe that

the funeral counselor should refer the individual to a quali-
fied therapist.

Through its counseling role, funeral service could
become a very effective referral vehicle, a vehicle which is
certainly needed and presently in complete disarray within
the medical profession as it relates to thanatology. This,
however, is easier said than done because problems do exist
when one seeks to find an appropriate therapist.

We know of experimentation by some therapists who were
not thanatologists, who have tried to shock their patients
out of grief and have failed. We know of others who have
tried to medicate away grief and have also failed. The
results have been not only failure to resolve grief but also
the problems of addiction. Referring a client carries with
it a serious responsibility. In good conscience, we cannot
refer our clients unless we are convinced that the therapist
knows the concerns of the dying and the bereaved and will not
subject the grieving to experimentation that we know has
failed.

Because many therapists refuse to recognize funeral
service practitioners as worthy professionals and counselors,
they refuse to associate with them. Consequently, those in
funeral service do not always know who is competent. Thanatology is experiencing a knowledge explosion. It is difficult
for caregivers to leave their base of operations and go out
of town to pick up some of this new information. Wanting to
improve their knowledge, the funeral directors in my town
decided to bring educational resources into town. It was
thought that in this way we would make this education available to all caregivers in the community and that all would
learn together. We recruited a panel of authorities in the
field of death, grief, bereavement, and the funeral to visit
with us. It was gratifying to see the unexpectedly large
number in attendance at the sessions held. The nurses, the
social workers, the agency directors, the case workers,
nursing students, high school students, educators, clergymen,
funeral directors, and other interested parties came. However, not a single psychiatrist came. Not a single psychologist came. Not a single medical doctor came. The seminars
were a success but would have been much more valuable if
medical professionals had not stayed home. They learned
nothing about our concerns, and they continue to suspect our
intentions.

We in funeral service receive not only the deceased
remains that leave the hospital or the nursing home. We also
receive the living remains that have left those institutions.
Fortunately, some survivors have been helped by the quality
of service that they have been given by some of the available
caregivers. But we have seen many who have been hurt by the
lack of attention or sensitivity to their needs. Education

is really needed by all who profess to care for the dying and the bereaved.

If we caregivers are to meet the expectations of those who come to us for help, we must:

1. learn to know each other better as caregivers;

2. learn to understand and respect what each of us has to offer and to understand that no one has it all;

3. learn where we all fit in the big picture of giving care to others;

4. learn how to develop a sense of security that will allow us to purge ourselves of petty jealousies, resentments, and suspicions that can impair our effectiveness.

With a spirit of cooperation, we can elevate the quality of service and care we are called upon to render, and the beneficiary of this will be the suffering who are counting on us to care enough.

15

A Philosophy of Caring for the Care-Giving Professional

Victor F. Scalise

The most important word in the caregiving professional's vocabulary is caring. There is no more important word or attitude. The key to helping a person in grief is caring.

At the time he was serving his apprenticeship in a funeral home, one of my students shared the following experience with me.

I was joined by a little girl whose grandfather was being waked in the funeral home. She was talkative, seemingly well adjusted, and about eight years of age. She felt left out of most of the family discussion going on in the chapel.

"They don't think I know," she said. "Grampie is dead. He died because he was very sick and had been ill for a long time."

She told me about the things she used to do with her grandfather, the places she alone had been with him and how much he had taught her.

"We used to play this game everytime I saw him. He would have packages of M & M's in his pocket and I would have to guess which one they were in."

The morning of the funeral, she made a special effort to see me. She said, "May I ask you a favor?" She then reached into her pocket and pulled out a package of M & M's and asked if I could put them in Grampie's pocket. "Sure," I replied and did just that. As she walked away she said, "He never went anywhere without them."

Listening, being responsive to the needs of others, even a little child. Doing the unorthodox, the unusual in the usual situation all are part of the help and healing called caring.

A woman whose husband died was asked by a funeral professional in Maine to write out a prescription for caring. She wrote in part:

> The showing of true concern is easily sensed. A hand-clasp, an arm around one's shoulders . . . just little personal contacts but so meaningful. Too often the bereaved feels like an untouchable, alone in a little plot with well-wishers standing around the perimeter making no tangible effort to reach her.
>
> A simple telephone call can break the unbearable silence of a home no longer shared. Better still, a short house call especially on a Sunday afternoon or in the evening, low emotional periods, would be so comforting. What can one say or not say at such times? Any honest words of encouragement for progress being made are like cool water to one athirst. Conversation of a quiet, contemplative nature, rather than of effusiveness or forced gaity, is welcome.
>
> Welcome, too, is repeated assurance that reactions to grief are not a lack of Christian belief and ideals. Male conversation and assurance are important to a widow who misses this deeply if her marriage has been one of day-to-day sharing with her mate.
>
> Occasionally, those who want to help, emphasize again and again, that, "You shouldn't be like this; you are being selfish; you are living an inward existence!" Bascially, this may be true, but hearing this viewpoint only causes one to become more depressed, thinking she is failing to live up to her own ideals or those cherished by her mate.
>
> Patience and more patience on the part of the helper is so desperately needed for reassuring the bereaved one, as she repeatedly dips into the wells of grief. . . . The prayers and personal concerns of others over an extended period of time can help build a bridge to new life.

A prescription for caring includes true concern, the personal touch, our presence, repeated assurances, being non-judgmental, patience and prayers not just for a day, a week, or a month but over an extended period of time. Dr. Robert S. Weiss of Harvard has stressed that loneliness does not come from being alone but from being deprived of needed relationships and the right company (1973).

A woman attended a widow-to-widow seminar sponsored by a funeral home in the greater Boston area. After the meeting she wrote me a letter:

> I saw my brother-in-law for a few minutes. He
> told me that I must start going out and find a
> boyfriend and have some sex, and that I must go on
> living. I cried and couldn't stop. I tried to
> make light of it, but he kept insisting this is
> the way. . . . I don't feel emotionally stable
> enough to think of anything like that. . . . I am
> still exhausted from the nearly two years of
> strain of caring for a husband dying of cancer.
> I feel I can hardly cope with my own feelings,
> much less with another's.

Caring is not the exploiting of a person who is vulnerable, either economically or emotionally. Caring is the courage to stand by others in trying circumstances, taking risks that go beyond safety and security (Mayeroff 1971).

In the spring of 1979 my father was diagnosed with an operable brain tumor. Our family took him into our home and cared for him as long as it was physically possible. During the last several months of his life, he required the assistance of an extended care facility.

In a Boston facility they restrained him in his chair for his physical security. In this efficient, well-run center everything was clean and antiseptic. Only one element was missing: genuine caring. In June, we moved our father to another extended care facility in Maine near our summer cottage. The nun at the Good Shepherd Villa asked what things my father liked. Among them was reading; he had a seven thousand book library. Now he was unable to read. But he also loved art and music. Within 24 hours our father had a headset playing the great symphonies he loved.

He was no longer on drugs except for the most essential ones. He was not restrained in his chair. The last two months of his life were peaceful and serene because the nuns at the Good Shepherd Villa were loving and caring. He died on the Sunday before Labor Day in an environment that others might characterize as hospice-like.

Evans has written the story of a man who is dying and the family's encounter with two doctors (1971). The surgeon was competent but coldly efficient, a man without sympathy or understanding. He sent his patient home to die of cancer. But one night the pain was so bad the family called upon a young resident who lived in their building. Although this was not his patient, he responded. Quietly, he questioned the patient. He reassured him as he spoke. The young resident gave him a gentle physical examination. The patient experienced dramatic relief. This was the first time he had been touched by another, except his wife, since he had left the hospital.

A caregiver may possess the most sophisticated physical and psychological tools. The most modern of facilities may be provided. But as the Apostle Paul states, "If you have not charity, you are nothing." The task of professional care-givers is not to fight over turf, argue about professional priority, denigrate one another's role, or quarrel about titles.

If we are really caregivers then we shall do precisely that as an interdisciplinary team of doctors, clergy, and funeral professionals. We will humble ourselves and offer genuine loving care to those in need. We shall do so with the unspoken word, the physical touch, true empathy. All this and more is not the private domain of the doctor, nurse, social worker, clergyperson, or funeral professional. It is not one group that serves. We have all been called to be healers of persons and our most useful gift is the spirit of caring. And the secret of caring for the person in acute grief is *caring* for the person.

REFERENCES

Evans, J. *Living with a Man Who Is Dying*. New York: Tap-linger, 1971.

Mayeroff, M. *On Caring*. New York: Harper and Row, 1971.

Weiss, R. *Loneliness*. Cambridge: The M.I.T. Press, 1973.

16

The Preparation of
a Crisis Counselor
for the Terminally Ill
and Their Families

Robert A. Hogan
and
Gerald A. Lienhart

The person who has endured tragedy has something to say
to the future counselor. Enrolled in the senior author's
behavior disorders class was a woman whose child had died
slowly over a long, cruel year. School became her individual
therapy, her attempt at personal growth and understanding.
Through her intervention, we placed an advanced graduate
student in an unusual educational experience: four families
who had lost a child or who, at the time, had a terminally
ill child became teachers for a portion of the junior author's
professional development as a crisis counselor. We believe
that this experience was extremely valuable and the families
rightly assumed that, through sharing their loss, they had
made a contribution.

We began the preparation of the crisis counselor by
having him read within the specialized area of dying. Con-
currently, he was given instructions on dealing with parents
in crisis and was supplied with a set of questions for a
semistructured interview.

Our goal was to provide the student with a nonstructured,
relaxed approach to the interview that would be conducive to
learning. However, inquiry into key areas was suggested. At
first, the student was advised to consider general questions
designed to facilitate emotional release and to aid in establishing rapport with the person. For example, questions such
as "How are things going?", "How do you feel?", "How is your
health?", "How did it happen?", or "Can you tell me how you
first found out?" were suggested. We invited inquiry into the
parent's perception of medical professionals and other medical
personnel. The family was asked to consider how the doctor
behaved during their ordeal and whether or not they had
encountered any problems in dealing with hospital personnel.
Questions about the improvement of hospital service and ways

in which the hospital staff might improve their relationships with the family were included.

Endless questions are possible when exploring family interrelationships. Generally, we examined how the family was affected by the crisis and the ways in which relationships between family members were altered. We attempted to explore difficulties with children, sacrifices of the family, unmet needs of the individuals, and ways in which professionals, in-laws, neighbors, or clergy might improve these conditions. We were very concerned about the inability of the person to function and about expressions of helplessness and hopelessness.

The parent's relationship with the deceased or terminally ill child was closely examined. Inquiry was made into the parents' responses to their sick child and things they wished they had done; we attempted to establish the nature of the parental emotional response. We asked, for example, if parents believed they could have done more for the child or if they should have done things differently. We requested information on the course of the child's illness and suffering. Questions related to the neighbors, friends, or in-laws were designed to explore the degree of emotional support or concrete assistance provided, to discover ways in which significant persons increased the problem, and to develop some guidelines for family assistance.

Because the goal of the project was student-counselor development, extensive questioning on this topic was advised. We asked family members for suggestions on student training and experiences and on background knowledge needed to counsel effectively. We asked what they considered to be important in development of the counselor and inquired about mistakes to be avoided.

We were concerned about the personal growth of family members and their orientation toward the future. Questions were proposed that delved into the importance of religion and belief, including how these beliefs provided support and how they were altered by the experience of losing a child. Our concerns were also for prior experience with death and its effect. Examination of the entire grief process was considered vital. Finally, we directed the parents' thoughts toward their future, through questions about what they had learned from their experience, how their lives had been altered, and what meaning they attached to the experience.

PROFESSIONAL PREPARATION

Selection of a mature student-counselor for advanced graduate school preparation through experiences with families who have transcended crisis or who are still attempting to resolve their conflict, is essential. Equally important to this specialized area of counseling is the academic orientation of the student. Reading was an intrinsic part of this program. These readings could be considered in implementing this crisis counselor technique: Kübler-Ross's 1969 and 1975 books, and the journals *Advances in Thanatology* and *Omega*, offer an excellent beginning orientation. Kron (1974) offers a popularized approach to the topic of dying and an introduction to the literature. *The Psychology of Death* (Kastenbaum and Aisenberg 1972) provides an extensive psychological view of the death concept, from dying to murder and suicide. Frankl (1962) and Imara (1975) examine both the meaning of life and of dying as a last stage of growth.

Carey's report (1975) on important principles derived from research investigation with terminally ill patients includes practical advice for patient care. Parkes (1970), who researched the grief process, gives the prospective counselor a long-term insight into the grief process.

Gordon and Kutner (1965) discuss the consequences of childhood illness and, in addition, examine the long-term effect of illness on parental conceptions, including parental problems of exclusion from the community, parental loss of rewards, and the effect of prolonged stress. Kessler (1966, pp. 191-96) has an excellent section on parental counseling in her book, which is applicable to varied categories of family conflict. Additionally, Chapter 13, the "mind-body" chapter, contains invaluable information on children's emotional reactions to illness, hospitalization, surgery, and physical disabilities.

The future clinician, though well grounded in theory through a text such as that by Patterson (1973), is often less prepared for crisis intervention. Barten's *Brief Therapies* (1971) and Resnik and Ruben's *Emergency Psychiatric Care* (1975) can help provide such preparation. In addition, four books devoted to the problems of dying and grief, each with sections on management of the child and the family, are those by Burton (1974), Schoenberg, Carr, Peretz, and Kutscher (1970), Schoenberg, Carr, Kutscher, Peretz, and Goldberg (1974), and Schowalter et al. (1983). These might well be considered as resource texts.

An especially appropriate selection would be Volkan's writings on grief therapy (1975). This technique, according to Volkan, is designed to aid individuals in bringing into awareness their memories of the deceased. The method allows a test of experiences against reality. Grief therapy is used to enable the bereaved to accept their emotions and to face the experience of death. Finally, implosive therapy (Hogan 1969; Stampfl 1967) is a therapeutic approach well suited to the release of emotion, and has been used in dealing with problems of guilt and hostility.

STUDENT OBSERVATIONS AND OPINIONS

The grieving families interviewed indicated that they had received the greatest support from ministers, but this still seemed to leave them dissatisfied. Ministers provided positive, but passive support. They often could not answer the families' philosophical questions about death and dying. Given this lack of complete satisfaction with ministerial counseling it was surprising to note that none of the families had experienced a negative change in their religious convictions.

Grieving families were frequently dissatisfied with their interactions with the medical profession, particularly doctors. They felt that many physicians took a cold, insensitive approach to them and to their grief. A physician's emotional involvement with the patient or family may make it personally painful to the doctor if a friend is in pain or dies.

The one area in which families expressed the most difficulty with physicians was in getting information about their child's illness and a prediction of what the child would go through. The parents often did not know whom to ask for additional information and often they did not know what to ask. It is my observation that some doctors only tell patients and families what they feel it is necessary for them to know. The families interviewed felt that physicians resented any further questioning. In the literature, Wiener (1970) suggests that when physicians break the news of a terminal illness to a family, they should be prepared to discuss the diagnosis, treatment, the course of the disease, and the prognosis. However, Wiener cautions that because of the shock of the revelation, families may not receive or remember all of the information. I believe that misperception and repression may also contribute to this family perception of the physician.

It was my impression that the families experienced a wide variety of conflicts as a result of the illness or death of their child. I believe it is important that the counselor identify the specific problem areas of each family. Most of the families interviewed experienced conflict over what and how to tell their dying child about the illness. All of the families indicated that they had experienced marital difficulties. Extra demands are always placed on both parents. It seemed to me that a portion of the marital discord came about from lack of communication.

My interviews indicated that fathers most often had the greatest difficulty in communicating their feelings. This finding is consistent with the research of Jourard (1964), which suggests that because of cultural training, males typically avoid exposing themselves psychologically to others, a condition that Jourard believes inhibits their emotional development. I believe that the fathers are particularly vulnerable during the trauma of death, not only because of their problems of expression, but also because they are unable to do anything constructive to improve the situation.

Other children in the family may also experience conflict as a result of the illness or death of a sibling. They may well have unresolved feelings that are unexpressed. Children may experience difficulties at school or with peers. Guilt is a common cause of conflict among children in the family. Rivalry between children is common, and negative feelings are often associated with a sibling's death. Children may believe that their negative feelings in some magical way caused their sibling to die. Sometimes children are not apprised of their sibling's condition or are not asked to share in the difficult family decisions. In addition, the stress of the situation and the financial demands it imposes can isolate parents from their other children. These problems are typical of those that occurred in the families studied.

Guilt can be a problem for any member of the family. Parents may feel that they did not give the child enough love or care. They often expressed the view that they should have done something different in the way of medical treatment. Frequently, they felt guilty about not having the financial resources to do more for the child. The terminal illness may become such a burden on the family that some members may wish death to occur soon, so they can get back to a more normal routine. This may take the form of anger toward the child and eventually produce guilt feelings after the child's death. When problems of this kind occur, it is probably desirable for family members to express their feelings to each other and work them through. Children may be relieved of guilt feelings by allowing them to contribute to the solution of them as productive family members. This can be construed as a family growth process.

All of the families who had lost a member to terminal illness experienced, as expected, an intense grief reaction. Family members often felt that the grief they were experiencing was insurmountable and would never end. It is important to try to help families understand that grief is a process. It has a beginning and an end, and it must be worked through in order to be resolved. It is an extinction-like process that the bereaved must go through in order to divest themselves of emotional attachment to others by reliving prior experiences through imagery and feelings. If the process is blocked by guilt, aggression, or ambivalent attachment to the deceased, the grief process will be prolonged.

Seligman (1975), writing on emotional development, depression, and death, made the point that when man cannot control an environment or lacks the ability to predict events, then helplessness, anxiety, depression, or even death may occur. What are the implications of Seligman's work for the counselor? I believe that the counselor must instruct parents about the many things they can do to deal with their anxiety and to avoid feelings of helplessness. For example, parents can provide school, home, and play environments that are as normal as circumstances allow. This can be particularly helpful during periods of remission in the sick child's disease. Another possibility is to encourage the growth of the bereaved by having them write down and explore their experiences about death, as suggested by Mize (1975).

FINAL PRINCIPLES AND COUNSELING CONSIDERATIONS

Prospective counselors must evolve as persons and face themselves in a number of crucial areas. In the metamorphosis, each counselor might ask these key questions: (1) Could I assist parents in informing other members of the family, often children, about the terminal illness or death of a family member? (2) Am I capable of aiding dying people by encouraging their families to be with them rather than leaving them in emotional isolation? Would I emotionally abandon the dying or will I provide comfort by assisting their families to discuss death openly? (3) If a dying person cannot relate to the family and does not even wish to speak to them, would I be willing to face this crisis? (4) The counselor must recognize the therapeutic value of catharsis and abreaction, but would I permit clients to direct their hostility toward me through displacement of their emotions? (5) Am I prepared to deal with suicide or other avoidance mechanisms of my clients? (6) Rapport is a sophisticated psychological term, but can I deal therapeutically with individuals I dislike, especially when they behave unkindly toward their dying children? (7) Parents are threatened by their child's impending death, for they are coming to grips with their own vulnerability, but can I, as a counselor, deal with my own feelings about my own inevitable death?

We believe that the crisis counselor should be able to provide supportive therapy. This may entail emotional commitment, but it may also include arranging free time for a parent. No person can face a crisis full-time. Denial and repression are common coping mechanisms. A counselor assists the individual to face truth. The ability to apply rational therapeutic skills in directing the client toward problem-solving is often a necessity, as is the ability to point out irrational behavior. In addition, counselors should be skilled in interpreting nonverbal behavior and listening with a "third ear" to the real message. This skill is essential to understanding the symbolic expressions of children.

We believe that the prospective counselor should be versed in the understanding of abnormal grief reactions, and should have insight into the causes of these behaviors. Blank (1969) observed that abnormal grief reactions can be associated with alcoholism, the death of a parent or sibling early in an individual's life, homosexuality, psychiatric hospitalization, a history of depressive reactions, prolonged conflict with the deceased, and marked dependency on the deceased. These conditions may require long-term psychiatric intervention.

Family counselors should be attuned to family conflict. Crisis for the family usually means loss of personal status, psychological vulnerability, resulting in dependency and escapism; anxiety; acute physical discomfort and psycho-physical disorders; feelings of being unloved and unwanted; restriction of personal freedom; and serious economic problems.

Finally, we believe that the counselor must transmit to clients faith in their own ability, in time, to solve personal conflict and that the dying person should be assisted in preserving his identity and dignity.

SUMMARY OF RECOMMENDATIONS

1. *Training.* We recommend affiliation with a hospital, especially one with an existing counseling service. Ideally, the student should have many natural interactions with various members of the families to be involved in the training project.

2. *Criteria for selecting trainees.* We recommend selection of mature graduate students near the end of their program (practicum level). We believe it is essential that students be widely read before making family contacts, and that they be given an opportunity to explore their own feelings and discuss counseling issues prior to interaction with families.

3. *Qualifications and/or experience of supervisors.* We believe that supervisors should be empathetic individuals who are willing to discuss the emotional issues and personal conflicts of trainees, not people who are oriented primarily toward academics. Supervisors should also be willing to respond to student conflict emerging from counselor-family contacts. Ideally, supervisors should have experience in death counseling themselves.

REFERENCES

Barten, H.H., ed. *Brief Therapies.* New York: Behavioral Publications, 1971.

Blank, H.R. "Mourning." In A.H. Kutscher, ed., *Death and Bereavement*, pp. 204-6. Springfield, Ill.: Charles C Thomas, 1969.

Burton, C., ed. *Care of the Child Facing Death*. London: Routledge and Kegan Paul, 1974.

Carey, R.G. "Living Until Death: A Program of Service and Research for the Terminally Ill." In E. Kübler-Ross, ed., *Death, The Final Stage of Growth*. Englewood Cliffs, N.J.: Prentice-Hall, 1975.

Frankl, V. *Man's Search for Meaning*. Boston: Beacon Press, 1962.

Gordon, N.B. and B. Kutner. "Long-Term and Fatal Illness and the Family." *Journal of Health and Human Behavior* 6 (1968), 190-96.

Hogan, R.A. "Implosively Oriented Behavior Modification, Therapy Considerations." *Behavior Research and Therapy* 7 (1969), 177-83.

Imara, M. "Dying as the Last Stage of Growth." In E. Kübler-Ross, ed., *Death, the Final Stage of Growth*. Englewood Cliffs, N.J.: Prentice-Hall, 1975.

Jourard, S.M. *The Transparent Self*. New York: Van Nostrand, 1964.

Kastenbaum, R. and R. Aisenberg. *The Psychology of Death*. New York: Springer, 1972.

Kessler, J.W. *Psychopathology of Childhood*. Englewood Cliffs, N.J.: Prentice-Hall, 1966.

Kron, J. "Learning to Live with Death." *Omega* 5 (1974), 5-24.

Kübler-Ross, E. *On Death and Dying*. New York: Macmillan, 1969.

---, ed. *Death, the Final Stage of Growth*. Englewood Cliffs, N.J.: Prentice-Hall, 1975.

Mize, E. "A Mother Mourns and Grows." In E. Kübler-Ross, ed., *Death, the Final Stage of Growth*. Englewood Cliffs, N.J.: Prentice-Hall, 1975.

Patterson, C.H. *Theories of Counseling and Psychotherapy*. New York: Harper and Row, 1973.

Parkes, C.M. "The First Year of Bereavement." *Psychiatry* 33 (1970), 444-67.

Resnik, H.L. and H.L. Ruben, eds. "Emergency Psychiatric Care." In *The Management of Mental Health Crises*. The National Institute of Mental Health, Bowie, Md.: Charles Press, 1975.

Schoenberg, B., A.C. Carr, A.H. Kutscher, D. Peretz, eds. *Loss and Grief: Psychological Management in Medical Practice*. New York: Columbia University Press, 1970.

--- et al., eds. *Anticipatory Grief*. New York: Columbia University Press, 1974.

Schowalter, J.E., P.R. Patterson, M. Tallmer, A.H. Kutscher, S.V. Gullo, and D. Peretz, eds. *The Child and Death*. New York: Columbia University Press, 1983.

Seligman, M.E. "Helplessness." In *On Depression, Development, and Death*. San Francisco: W. H. Freeman, 1975.

Stampfl, T.G. and D.J. Levis. "Essentials of Implosive Therapy, A Learning Theory Based on Psychodynamic Behavioral Therapy." *Journal of Abnormal Psychology* 6 (1967), 496-503.

Volkan, V.D. "More on Re-Grief Therapy." *Journal of Thanatology* 3 (1975), 77-91.

Wiener, J. "Reaction of the Family to the Fatal Illness of a Child." In B. Schoenberg et al., eds., *Loss and Grief: Psychological Management in Medical Practice*, pp. 87-107. New York: Columbia University Press, 1970.

17

The Effect of
Counseling Skills Training
on the Expression of Empathy
by Funeral Directors

Ronald E. Troyer

Is there a difference in the expression of empathy by
funeral directors who have had counseling skills training and
those who have not had this training? To determine if this
is so, a forced-answer survey was distributed to a sample of
funeral directors graduated from the Cincinnati College of
Mortuary Science. The results indicate significant statisti-
cal differences between these groups in the degree of empathy
expressed. The group that had no counseling skills training
was in almost unanimous agreement that such training is
important and necessary.

INTRODUCTION

In September 1977, the Cincinnati College of Mortuary
Science introduced counseling principles and procedures into
its curriculum as required coursework for its students.
This additional training was deemed necessary as a result
of several long-term studies indicating the need for counseling and communications skills training for future funeral
directors (Curriculum Study Committee Report 1974; Fitzsimmons 1977). It was presumed that the counseling skills
training would cause funeral service practitioners to become
more aware of and sensitive to the feelings of their clients.
The purpose of the research program was to find if there is
a difference in the expression of empathy by funeral directors who have had counseling skills training as compared to
funeral directors who have not had this training.
The need for bereavement counseling in our present
society has been established by a number of researchers
(Fulton 1976; Lindemann 1944; Steele 1977). Our technology
has created a health care system in which death is not

readily seen or observed. When experiencing a death, today's smaller nuclear family may "never have had a direct contact with a professional caregiving person other than a funeral director" (Mayes 1979, p. 32). In the last decade, funeral directors have become increasingly aware of the counselor role that is available to them. Raether and Slater, in their book *The Funeral Director and His Role as a Counselor*, quote Dr. Edgar Jackson, a noted pastoral psychologist: "Funeral directors do not choose as to whether or not they will be counselors. Their only choice is will they be a good or bad counselor?" (Raether and Slater 1975, p. 1). Others have reinforced the need for funeral directors to be able to fill such a role (Margolis et al. 1981). Responsible funeral directors are realizing that what they do has immense therapeutic value to those who suffer the loss of a loved one. Nichols (1975), a funeral director, writes that it is necessary for funeral directors to move from the role of a functionary to that of a facilitator. Nichols also says:

> *The role of professionals, neighbors, and community is to bring gentle intervention and confrontation with reality and to ease reality upon a mind which seeks to reject reality. Real, genuine, and authentic feelings must have an early opportunity for expression and ventilation. It is a well accepted psychological premise that serious attempts to delay or avoid grief work only increase the possibility of a poor adjustment. The real work of the death professional, the death ritual, and those who enter into the caring of the dying and the grieving is to give consent for mourning and to facilitate the grief work* [1975, p. 6].

PROCEDURES

A random sample survey was made of two groups of graduates from the Cincinnati College of Mortuary Science. The experimental group included only those who received the counseling skills training that was introduced into the curriculum in 1977. The control group included graduates from the two years preceding the teaching of a counseling skills course. There were approximately 160 graduates available in each group. Eighty randomly selected persons in each group were mailed a 15-item instrument designed to assess the level of empathy being expressed by the individual practitioner. There was also included a personal data sheet, a cover letter, and a stamped, self-addressed return envelope.

The instrument has a forced-choice answer to 15 specific situations a funeral director can expect to face. The five

available answers are based on Carkhuff's (1969) five levels
of empathetic understanding. A level-one response indicates
no understanding or feeling for the client; a level-five
response indicates a high level of understanding and empathy
for the client. (See Appendix A for an additional description of these five levels.) Content validity for the instrument was established by having the instrument evaluated and
the responses rated by three Ph.D.'s in Guidance and Counseling. In addition, a selected group of six funeral directors
in the Cincinnati area participated in a field study of the
instrument. Examination by these groups assisted in the
elimination of ambiguous items, unclear directions for mark-
ing, and other factors that might have detracted from the
usefulness of the survey instrument.

The personal data sheet was purposely placed last in the
four-page instrument. This was done to reduce the possibility
that respondents might be influenced to answer the 15 items
in a predisposed manner. The use of a mailed written survey
may have allowed the respondents to answer in what they feel
is a "socially desirable" manner as compared to what they
might say in a real-life situation. Although this researcher
considers this to be a limitation, there seems to be no other
practical manner in which to collect the data required. It
is assumed that the sample surveyed is characteristic of
funeral directors who have graduated from other accredited
mortuary science colleges over the same period of time.

RESULTS

The cover letter attached to the instrument included a
deadline of two weeks for the return of the instrument. A
total of 41 instruments were received from the control group
(no training). The experimental group of 80 subjects returned
a total of 51 instruments for a 64 percent return rate.

The data returned produced some very interesting findings in three areas:

1. The mean scores and their relationship to the
   Carkhuff scale at level three were significant.
   Level three is considered to be the minimum
   facilitative level to counsel effectively.

2. The 15 items in the instrument were constructed
   to cover five subject areas commonly found in
   bereavement counseling. These subject areas are
   Denial, Anger, Bargaining, Guilt, and Acceptance.
   There was a significant difference between the
   two groups of respondents in two subject areas.

3. The last three questions on the personal data
   sheet produced the interesting finding that

there is a strong, almost overwhelming agreement in both groups on the need to acquire and
use counseling skills in their work.

THE MEAN SCORES

The mean score of the control group was 45.6 as compared
to a mean score of 51.3 for the experimental group. The difference of mean scores between the groups was statistically
very significant ($t = 4.12$, $p < .001$). The difference of 5.7
in the mean scores can be readily seen in Table 17.1 when
comparing the frequency of the scores to the level-three
response necessary to facilitate a counseling relationship.
The experimental group, which received the counseling skills
training, placed the majority of their scores (82 percent)
in the level-three and level-four response areas. The control group, which received no counseling skills training,
placed only 51 percent at the level-three response score and
no one in the control group scored in the level-four response
area.

Table 17.1

Comparing Frequency of Scores to the
Level-Three Response

65–69		
60–64		Level-4 Response
55–59	Experimental	
50–54	Group ($N = 51$)	
45–49		Level-3 Response*
40–44	Control Group	
35–39	($N = 41$)	
30–34		Level-2 Response
5	10	15
	Frequency of Scores	

*Minimum facilitative level

Table 17.2 shows a significant difference in the percentage of scores under 45 for the control group (49 percent)
as compared to the experimental group (18 percent). A level-
two response score on the survey instrument would indicate
the funeral director is showing a poor understanding of the
client's expressions and overlooking some of the client's
deeper feelings.

Table 17.2

Percentage of Scores Above and Below 45
(Level-3 Response)

Scores	Control Group ($N = 41$)	Experimental Group ($N = 51$)
45 and over	51%	82%
Under 45	49%	18%

FIVE SUBJECT AREAS COVERED BY
THE INSTRUMENT

The 15 situations used in the instrument were purposely
designed to cover five subject areas common to bereavement
counseling. Table 17.3 shows the subject areas as well as
the percentage of response at each level. The control and
experimental groups both did well at handling situations that
concerned Denial, Bargaining, and Acceptance. Although the
experimental group did a little better in these three subject
areas, the difference was small enough not to be of real
significance. In these three areas, the funeral directors
all responded at level three or better most of the time.
    The noticeable difference between the groups was found
in the subject areas dealing with Anger and Guilt. The
control group clearly had a difficult time dealing with a
situation that involved an expression of anger by the client.
Nearly half of the responses by the control group were at
level two or level one. The experimental group did con-
siderably better, with half of their responses to anger at
levels four and five. The control group had almost as much
difficulty handling situations where guilt was expressed:
44 percent of the control group responded at level two and
level one, whereas the experimental group placed 48 percent
of their responses at levels four and five. Clearly, the
control group, which did not have counseling skills training,

had a more difficult time handling expressions of anger and guilt. The experimental group, which had received counseling skills training, demonstrated a high degree of understanding and acceptance of expressions of anger and guilt.

Table 17.3

Subject Areas and Percentage of Responses
in Each Level

Subject Area	Level				
Group*	1	2	3	4	5
Denial					
Control	3%	5%	49%	35%	7%
Experimental	2	3	64	20	11
Anger					
Control	34	13	24	12	17
Experimental	16	14	19	32	19
Bargaining					
Control	5	19	18	22	36
Experimental	4	12	23	18	43
Guilt					
Control	29	14	25	21	11
Experimental	14	16	22	33	15
Acceptance					
Control	9	24	29	20	18
Experimental	6	15	25	19	35

*Control Group: (N = 41); Experimental Group: (N = 51).

PERSONAL DATA SHEET RESULTS

The personal data sheet was used to determine to which group the returned instrument belonged. Additional information about employment and the nature of work being done was also requested. The data collected in questions one through five produced no significant findings. The data from questions six, seven, and eight showed strong agreement by the two groups as to the need for counseling skills by the funeral director. Table 17.4 shows the percentage of responses by the two groups to the three questions. In question six, the experimental group agreed 100 percent that counseling skills should be taught in a mortuary science college. The control group strongly agreed (88 percent) that such a course should be taught.

Table 17.4

Personal Data Sheet Responses
in Percentages

Control Group (*N* = 41)		Experimental Group (*N* = 51)

6. Do you feel there is a need to teach counseling skills to students in the mortuary science colleges?

73%	Yes, as a required subject	96%
15	Yes, as an elective subject	4
12	No	0

7. Would you, *if given the opportunity*, take a course in *Counseling Principles & Procedures* at a college or university near you?

83%	Yes	98%
17	No	2

8. An important part of the future of funeral service will depend upon funeral directors becoming, through proper training, capable and concerned counselors.

49%	Strongly agree	59%
37	Agree	41
12	Disagree	0
2	Strongly disagree	0

Question seven asked respondents if they would take a counseling skills course at a college near them, if given the opportunity. Of the experimental group, 98 percent answered affirmatively even though they had already had such course work within the last two years. Typical of the reasons given was, "The more I know about counseling the better I'll be as

a counselor." The control group responded strongly in the
affirmative (83 percent) that they would take a counseling
skills course if given the opportunity. They are indicating
a strong desire to acquire training in counseling skills at
the college level.

Question eight gave the two groups an opportunity to
express their belief in the importance that counseling skills
would have for funeral directors in the future. The experimental group agreed 100 percent that an important part of the
future of funeral service depended on funeral directors
becoming properly trained counselors. Of those in the control group, 86 percent believe the same, even though they had
not had formal training as counselors. There was nearly
unanimous agreement by the two groups that counseling skills
should be taught and used in professional practice.

DISCUSSION

The intent of this research was to determine whether or
not counseling skills training has an effect on the expression
of empathy by funeral directors. From the results, one can
conclude that there is certainly enough of a difference
between those who have had such training and those who have
not to merit the continuation of a counseling skills course
at the Cincinnati College of Mortuary Science. Those funeral
directors who have received counseling skills training demonstrated an ability to respond at a higher level of empathetic
understanding. Providing such training as part of the total
education of prospective funeral directors seems logically to
be the responsibility of mortuary science colleges. Health
care professionals will continue to call for formal education
in counseling for funeral directors (*The American Funeral
Director* 1979; Oman 1980). Future funeral directors who do
not receive this training will face a struggle to maintain
"professional" status. It is important that the education
available to these funeral directors prepare them not only
for the present, but also for the future responsibilities
they must assume.

The conclusive agreement of the two groups that counseling skills should be acquired and used in practice may be more
an indication of the ages of the individuals in this sample
than of anything else. The funeral directors in this study
were recent graduates. They are, for the most part, under 25
years of age and not far removed from academic life. The
findings of this study, that counseling skills training makes
a positive difference, can safely be applied to the general
population of funeral directors who finished college within
the last five years. In fact, this researcher speculates that
the same or more significant results would be found if the

entire population of funeral service directors were surveyed.
At present, however, there are no data to support this speculation. It would be necessary to collect data from funeral
directors at all age levels and who finished school ten, 20,
or 30 years ago in order to determine the effects of their
years of experience on their ability to respond empathetically
to the situations presented in the survey instrument used in
this study. If this were done and the results were as significant as those obtained in this study, the importance of
offering continuing education courses in counseling could not
be ignored.

There is no doubt that a need exists for larger and more
extensive studies in this area. The extent to which funeral
directors will serve as bereavement counselors in the future
will partially depend upon the availability of research
material to support or refute the necessity of this role.

REFERENCES

Carkhuff, R. *Helping and Human Relations: A Primer for Lay
and Professional Helpers*, Vols. I and II. New York:
Holt, Rinehart and Winston, 1969.

*Curriculum Study Committee Report to the American Board of
Funeral Service Education*, 1974.

Fitzsimmons, D. "Objectives in Training Embalmers—Funeral
Directors for the Future." *Champion Expanding Encyclo-
pedia of Mortuary Practice*. Springfield, Ohio: Champion
Company, 1977.

Fulton, R., ed. *Death and Identity*. New York: John Wiley
and Sons, 1976.

"How Other Professionals View the American Funeral and the
Funeral Director." *The American Funeral Director* 102
(August 1979), 20-22.

Lindemann, E. "Symptomatology and Management of Acute Grief."
American Journal of Psychiatry 101 (1944), 141-48.

Mayes, P. "Because of You—Someone's Tomorrow Will be Better."
The Director 10 (October 1979), 32-35.

Margolis, O.S., H.C. Raether, A.H. Kutscher, J.B. Powers,
I.B. Seeland, R. DeBellis, and D.J. Cherico, eds. *Acute
Grief: Counseling the Bereaved*. New York: Columbia
University Press, 1981.

Nichols, R. "Rationale for Death Education--Social/Psycho-
    logical Viewpoint." Paper presented at Symposium on
    Death Education, Ohio State University, Columbus, Ohio,
    November 8, 1975.

Oman, J.B. "How Adequate Is Funeral Service Education?" *The
    Dodge Magazine* 72 (January 1980), 20-21.

Raether, H.C. and R.J. Slater. *The Funeral Director and His
    Role as a Counselor.* Milwaukee: National Funeral
    Directors Association, 1975.

Schulman, E. *Intervention in Human Services.* St. Louis:
    C. V. Mosby, 1978.

Steele, D. "The Counselor's Response to Death." *Personnel
    and Guidance Journal* 56 (November 1977), 164-67.

APPENDIX A

SCALE FOR RATING FUNCTIONING LEVEL OF EMPATHY*

Level 1. Counselor responds in a distant and unrelated manner. Counselor shows little awareness even of client's obvious feelings. Counselor may try to understand, but only from his own viewpoint.

Level 2. Counselor shows poor understanding of the meaning of client's expressions. Counselor often responds accurately to client's obvious (surface) feeling but overlooks the depth of client's feelings.

Level 3. Counselor accurately responds with understanding of client's obvious feeling but does not realize how intensely client feels about some of the material discussed. Counselor may misinterpret deeper feelings.

Level 4. Counselor is sensitive to client's obvious and deeper feelings and accurately communicates his understanding to client, thus enabling the client to express feelings he was unable to talk about previously. Counselor tries to see things through client's eyes.

Level 5. Counselor accurately responds to client's obvious and most painful feelings. Counselor is tuned in to client's deeper feelings, but is not burdened or distressed by them. Counselor appreciates the meaning and importance of client's experiences.

---

*Schulman 1978, pp. 213-14.

18

An Overview
from the Perspective of a
Funeral Service Practitioner

Sumner James Waring, Jr.

The grief continuum exists as one of the most meaningful forums within which caregivers and educators in all
disciplines have opportunities to unite and grow in service
to human needs. Interdisciplinary colleagueship challenges
us to respond in multiple and meaningful ways. Sensitivity
to the needs of people who depend upon our skills expands
our required professional expertise and the opportunities
for working with each other on behalf of others. Our own
expectations of ourselves and consumer expectations of us
must anchor our focus.

I hail from within the profession of funeral service.
My observations have evolved from experiences in my practice
and from my experiences in working with and observing my
colleague disciplines. We share relevance, each in our own
way. Our common bond is the challenge to be people-sensi-
tive practitioners and human beings.

No matter what our discipline, we are interrelated as
functionaries within the service support system oriented
specifically toward people-care that enhances the quality
of life. This very quality of life is significantly proportionate to our abilities, as colleagues, to satisfactorily
fulfill consumer needs and expectations with mutual appreciation and respect. This is the foundation upon which we
must build.

Our individual competence within whichever discipline
we choose to practice must be directly proportionate to our
completeness as human beings. Our competence must be proportionate to a realistic view of ourselves, our individual
strengths and weaknesses, a realistic view of life itself,
ever acknowledging that we are placed on earth in this service; however, our individual persuasions may identify and

pursue such acknowledgment. Our comprehension, appreciation, and support of the aims, objectives, and skills practiced by those within colleague, caregiving, and educational disciplines, together with sensitivity to, knowledge about, respect for, and appreciation of the consumer wants and needs that we all strive to satisfy are essential to our completeness as human beings.

My purpose, using my profession as the example with which I am intimately familiar and about which I speak with authority, is to demonstrate the working of this web, to inspire those within my colleague disciplines to do similarly.

All who now function within a realm of death awareness are possessed to some greater or lesser degree by many of the consumers for whom they care. Indeed, sadly, consumer familiarity with this subject sometimes exceeds that possessed by many within our colleague disciplines. Knowledge explosion and consumerism within our time have resulted in less and less consumer reluctance to ask questions and to learn more about death, dying, grief, and all the remifications.

Funeral service practitioners are well aware of the fact that there is no eraser on decisions made by survivors when death-care becomes necessary. It is no time for the less knowledgeable, the less experienced, to be advising and acting. The ramifications of careless involvement and bad advice based on inadequate knowledge and societal pressures from uninformed lay persons can be overwhelmingly negative to survivors. While it is not our need or our responsibility to possess in-depth knowledge about and experience in others' areas of training and expertise, as intelligent, educated, skilled appreciators of each other, of what each does and attempts to do well, it is our obligation to recognize interrelated roles and their value and to refer to and depend on each other as we function complementarily to each other, not as rivals or detractors of each other. Those functioning within colleague disciplines are served well when they realize the intensification of consumer expectation as to general familiarity with the realm of death care, ceremony, and tributization as part of managing life wisely and well.

Acknowledgment and support of the funeral service functionary as the individual most familiar with and experienced in informing and counseling the consumer concerning all options and their ramifications pertaining to the death of a loved one, or pertaining to the seeking of knowledge in advance of one's own death in order to do what one perceives as being helpful to potential survivors, it seems to me, serves the best interests of that consumer. We can agree that such interests are not served well by the inexperienced or those offering and advancing only less meaningful, less responsible alternatives.

For many years funeral service practitioners have been expected to possess, and have possessed, meaningful orien-

tation toward, knowledge about, appreciation of, and respect
for the functions of colleague disciplines and the practitioners within them. If such trust is unwarranted, we have
an obligation to be part of the solution, not a continuation
and compounding of the problem however minor or severe it
might be.

Within the grief continuum, there has been a lifetime
of meaningful, satisfactory relationship between families and
funeral service practitioners that has enormous meaning and
value as knowledge about progress through the loss of great-
grandparent, grandparent, parent, husband/wife/child and
significant others is shared. Changing perceptions within
the family and society regarding not only our discipline of
service at time of death, but also of other disciplines are
evolving. Certain questions now call for responses:

- Will a modification of consumer wants and needs
  evolve? Has it already evolved? Should it have
  evolved if it has or has not?

- How does this relate to our respective perceptions of self and our responsibility and to the
  consumer's perception of same?

- How does one's ethnic background enter into the
  picture today?

- Where is religion in the web of family life?
  Where has it gone and why? How does whatever
  has happened to it relate to us? Will it affect
  what we do or our need for doing it?

- What *is* caregiving; are we all being as genuine
  as we can be in the defining and then giving of
  it?

- How can we help ourselves?

- Is money really *the* god, is it a god, or is it
  a careless crutch to the consumer, as well as
  practitioners within all disciplines? Dare we
  destroy this crutch? Or is it necessary for
  those who possess it to continue walking with it?

- What then is the "big picture" which our service
  system supports?

Long-term continuing loss is the "big picture" with which we
all deal, death-care functionaries in particular. One after
another, generation after generation, there has been the need
for the functionary whose knowledge and experience are primarily oriented toward helping survivors from the time noti-
fication of the death is received and responsibility for the
dead human body is entrusted to someone *until responsibility*

for it is accepted by those tending to its ultimate dis-
position, and thereafter to help survivors address and deal
with the events and experiences affecting the living.
There is need for knowledge to continue being compiled
within the responsible "house" our practices provide, as
well as to be imparted to others under the umbrella of
service to humankind. There is no telling what benefits
may emerge from the sharing of perspective, expertise and
experience.

   History is the basis of knowledge and understanding
and a stimulus toward the expansion of knowledge. Appreciation rather than deprecation of those who share a bond of
service is essential. There is no escaping the impact and
ramifications of death and grief on survivors. An understanding of the grief continuum is essential to the interdisciplinary colleagueship and growth which it is our united
responsibility to achieve in the best interests of consumer
America, as we join to translate potential into performance.

19

The Social Work Practitioner
and the Bereaved Client

Joan M. Danto

INTRODUCTION

Social work has long been a profession that focuses on
helping people to cope with various life situations. This is
reflected in the number of social service agencies that
provide help for individuals seeking housing, jobs, food,
and various other types of assistance. In addition, social
workers are found in community mental health agencies,
medical facilities, schools, and a variety of private and
community agency settings. There are also many social workers who are in private clinical social work practices. This
paper will attempt to describe such a practice as it relates
to treatment of bereaved clients.

Preparation in terms of education, one's own confrontation with death, and the sometime feelings of professional
isolation in relation to this aspect of treatment are issues
that will be discussed.

When I was a student, many social problems were discussed, issues raised, and possible solutions suggested.
Although, as future social workers, we were also taught to
help the clients where they were, this seldom referred to
bereaved clients. There were isolated comments or references
to dying patients, particularly if a student was in a hospital placement, but no direct teaching was offered on this
subject. It was almost as if there was a purposeful omission,
as if to suggest that it is impossible to cover all areas of
human problems.

Indeed, few related professional schools offered then
(or do now) programs to prepare their students for working in
this area. Why should this be? One explanation may be that
in spite of the fact that social workers are trained to meet
many societal needs, there is a strong avoidance of the area

of death. Perhaps it reflects the fear and denial of death
in society and in individuals.

In order for material of this sort to be included in
the curriculum, instructors must be convinced of the necessity for its inclusion. Two conditions must be met in order
for this material to be successfully taught: teachers must
be relatively free of anxiety about their own death and
dying; and students, supported by the teacher as a role model,
must be helped to examine and communicate their own fears
and anxieties about death (Miller 1977). This can be accomplished when there is a meaningful, trusting student/teacher
relationship that enables students to discuss conflict-laden
feelings. The purpose of this relationship is the enhance-
ment of students' self-awareness so that they can subsequently help their clients.

Kübler-Ross (1969) has proved that seminars are valuable
as a teaching method: "Participants speak freely about their
own reactions and fantasies in relation to the patient and
thus learn something about their own motivations and behaviors" (p. 266). Films can also be a useful educational tool
in helping students confront their own feelings about death.
Discussion handled gently and with understanding encourages
the realization that self-awareness does not mean the elimination of feelings about loss and death, but rather understanding a human condition. It is hoped that with this
knowledge, coping skills, and empathy, students can be prepared to become involved with their clients, but remain
separate from their bereavement.

As practicing social workers, we are frequently confronted with bereaved clients or ones who are suffering from
unresolved grief. It is then that we discover the need to
understand, to help our clients cope with their situations,
and to assist them in the resolution of their problems.

Most social workers are employed in agencies such as
child guidance clinics, schools, hospitals, cancer founda-
tions, family service agencies, or community mental health
agencies. Their clients may come to them for treatment
because that agency specializes in their particular problem
area. Within such agencies, there are usually opportunities
for professionals to interact, take coffee breaks and lunch
hours together and share a common feeling of camaraderie in
their professional life. They have frequent opportunities
to share problems or anxieties about clients. There is time
to ventilate feelings and to share information.

This is in marked contrast to the private clinical social
worker. Her practice may involve people who are suffering
from a variety of problems. If a client is referred who suffers from cancer or alcoholism, the social worker is not
likely to say, "I don't treat cancer patients," or "I don't
treat alcoholics." The social worker is likely to include

these people along with families whose trouble arises from the possibility of divorce or death. If the private practice social worker is treating a bereaved client, there is usually no other professional with whom to share this stressful situation. Although there are meetings and conferences to attend, the day-to-day practice is generally devoid of such contact unless the social worker is employed by a private clinic, hires a supervisor, or works closely with a thanatologically oriented physician.

Shortly after I had entered the practice of social work, a client suffering from chronic depression was referred to me. My education in social work had done little to prepare me to treat this client. However, here I was, a recent graduate ready to "cure the world." Even though my education had neglected to prepare me for this client, there was a fortunate difference for me: I had been attending thanatology meetings for years, and am married to a psychiatrist who specializes in this field.

CLINICAL MATERIAL

The client, Mrs. B, was a white married woman, 52 years old. She had a daughter, age 28. She had also had a son, but he had committed suicide two years earlier. She was extremely depressed and having thoughts of suicide. She was still grieving over the loss of her son. Her marriage had been stormy and the problems between Mrs. B and her husband were exacerbated by the death of their son.

According to her husband, she had always been provocative, causing problems with his family and ultimately driving their children away. (Their daughter lives out of town.) They both discussed the fact that for the first sixteen years of their marriage, Mrs. B was primarily responsible for raising their children. Mr. B assumed a passive role until their daughter told him that she resented his lack of involvement. This resulted in a close father-daughter relationship. Mrs. B had then felt "frozen out" by them.

To add to this painful situation, they became aware of their son's homosexuality around the time of his high school graduation. He often taunted his mother by acting in an exaggeratedly effeminate way. He finally decided to move to California. The father again placed the blame on her for "pushing" their son away.

When their son committed suicide, she was overwhelmed with guilt. It had been almost impossible for her to accept his homosexuality, but the suicide was more devastating. By the time she was referred to me, two years later, she was still guilt-ridden and suffering from pathologic grief.

My task was to help her resolve grief feelings, learn to relate more appropriately to her family, and accept the

fact that she was entitled to live and enjoy her life. I
felt it was important to help her hold her son responsible
for his decision to commit suicide. It was part of the
therapeutic task to help her achieve this because she had
not been able to hold him responsible in his lifetime.

The B's marriage relationship has improved somewhat.
Mrs. B and her husband are able to talk things out together.
One of her complaints had been that he never talked about
his business with her. He is now doing this, and it makes
her feel more accepted. Her daughter calls her frequently,
and their relationship has greatly improved. She has a
grandson now, and can share in this excitement with her family.

Mrs. B made significant progress in another way. For
a time she had a part-time job in a boutique. She had never
worked before and it was a gratifying experience. Unfortunately, the job ended after a holiday period when sales
decreased.

There are still many problems to resolve, but Mrs. B
has come a long way. When she is home alone, thoughts of her
son abound, but she is learning to handle these feelings.
I expect that in time she will learn to cope with life in a
more appropriate and successful way.

*   *   *

Mrs. R, a white, 55-year-old widow with a 24-year-old
son, was referred to me one month after her husband's death.
She was overwhelmed with grief, unable to see a future for
herself without her husband or even to cope with everyday
household tasks.

Both Mrs. R and her husband were born and raised in the
East. Mr. R was active in a political organization that
wanted to develop membership in the Midwest. As a result,
they moved to Detroit and away from both their families. Mrs.
R had grown up in an extremely unhappy home and was grateful
for the opportunity to move. However, once in Detroit, her
husband became increasingly occupied with his political
activities and spent long hours away from home. Mrs. R sus-
pected that he was seeing another woman and she herself
became involved with another party member. This person was
kind to her when she was feeling vulnerable because she had
no other relatives here. She subsequently became pregnant by
this man, who was black. Her husband accepted the child and
raised him as his own. This child was their only child.

Mrs. R's husband had recently died following kidney
transplant surgery. Although he had elected surgery over
dialysis, she felt guilty for not insisting on this treatment.
A teacher, she had been involved in a school project shortly
before he became ill and, after his death, blamed herself

for not being more available. The husband had always played
a dominant role in their marriage, and usually insisted on
having his way. At his death, she was totally unprepared to
manage her life.

School was scheduled to begin in a month. Even though
she was overwhelmed with grief, I felt that my immediate task
was to help her resume teaching. In my view, she needed to
commit herself to life and the day-to-day reality of caring
for herself and her son in order to discover her own power.
Another important aspect of treatment was to point out that
her husband's death was really one he chose. In spite of her
pleadings, he would not have accepted dialysis.

She had always been the one most responsible for raising
their son, so it was natural for her to turn to him and
attempt to maintain control. Although he was content to have
her care for his daily needs, such as food and laundry, he
began to resent her somewhat interfering attempts in his life.
He is a musician, and may ultimately take a job that involves
moving to another community. The treatment focus has shifted
to helping Mrs. R to allow her son to move, guilt-free, and
for her to seek new directions for her life. When we discuss
his possible move, she prefers to avoid dealing with the
issue until she is actually confronted with it.

Recently, she told me proudly that she had made arrangements for activities that she would begin this spring. Much
of her depression had lifted, but it must be pointed out that
she and her husband had always had few friends and no relatives in this area. Moving forward toward her single involvement is an extremely important positive step.

*   *   *

Mr. C is a 40-year-old white, married male. Both he and
his wife had been previously married. Eleven years ago, when
Mr. and Mrs. C married, she had two sons and he had a four-
year-old daughter. His now 15-year-old daughter was killed
in an automobile accident about one month before he was
referred to me.

Mr. C was the second eldest in a large family and had
always been a strong, "take charge" person on whom his family
could rely. He was a sports enthusiast and often played
basketball with neighbors. Friends were frequently at his
home, visiting or playing cards. His reading material generally included books of self-improvement.

Mr. C is employed in the sanitation department of a
large automobile plant. At the time of his daughter's death,
he was working on the day shift. The accident occurred when
his daughter and friend were returning from an evening swim
in a nearby lake. They were walking on the shoulder of the
road when a car making a right turn swerved to the opposite

side, hitting her and driving off. Subsequent investigation indicated that the driver had been drinking, that he had not turned on the headlights, and that he had left the scene of the accident.

Because the accident occurred near his home when Mr. C was informed, he rushed to the scene. When I first saw him, he was depressed, having difficulty working, and could not shake the image of his daughter immediately after being hit. Apparently, there had been considerable swelling, which distorted her looks. This was a particularly painful sight for him.

Treatment involved offering him an opportunity to talk about his daughter and ventilate angry feelings directed toward the driver. He was able to discuss his daughter and how much he missed her. Being basically religious, he felt somewhat at peace with the conviction that he might see her again someday.

After a few months, he was able to return to work. However, because of economic conditions, the factory cut back to two shifts and he was changed to the night shift. This changed his whole life-style. He was unable to spend time with friends, because they worked during the day. In addition, his wife was left home alone for long periods. The most difficult aspect was being away during the hour at which the accident occurred. He felt closed in, as if he wanted to escape. This made it impossible for him to continue working and he re-entered treatment. We discussed his depression during work and a possible change to the afternoon shift. As of now, he has returned to work and made a satisfactory adjustment.

*   *   *

Mrs. L is a 30-year-old black, divorced mother of four children. A nine-year-old daughter died one month before she was referred to me.

Mrs. L was born and raised in a southern state. She is the eldest of two daughters. Her parents had little money, so she left school at age 13 to work in a cotton field. Four years after an early marriage, she and her husband separated and she moved up north to work. She had two children who stayed with a grandmother when she left. She subsequently had three other children.

She felt close to all her children and wanted to be a good mother. Mrs. L was concerned about their health and welfare. When her nine-year-old daughter had a broken arm that mended poorly, she agreed to corrective surgery for the child.

In preparation for surgery, an overdose of medication was administered and her daughter went into brainstem depres-

sion, which resulted in her eventual death. According to
Mrs. L, the hospital authorities had been untruthful and
shunted her out of the way, refusing to explain any complications to her and leaving her feeling very much ignored.

Without her knowledge, the hospital authorities made
arrangements to send her daughter to a local children's
hospital for more specialized care. She was actually clin-
ically dead, but was kept on machines for two additional
days. By the time her child died, Mrs. L was completely
drained.

When I began treating her, she was consumed with grief.
She felt an aching loss and the feeling that she had failed
to protect her child. She was having difficulty caring for
her remaining family, was having severe sleep disturbance,
and could hardly eat.

Treatment involved giving her an opportunity to grieve.
Talking about the circumstances of her daughter's death
helped her to ventilate angry, impotent feelings directed
toward the hospital and staff. Sometimes it was important
to sit, hold her hand, and let her cry. Providing a comfortable, warm atmosphere in which she could relax helped
her feel that someone cared. In addition, when she felt
especially depressed, she was able to call me on the phone
and talk about her feelings. It was important to be available to her in this way. Part of my task was to point out
to her that she had done the responsible thing by attempting
to have the deformed arm reset properly. It was left to the
medical team to carry out their responsibility for the cor-
rection. She was not responsible for the death.

As time passed, she could accept this and began to set
her life in order. She decided to return to school for a
G.E.D. She is cooking meals and taking an active role with
her family. At present, she is on medical leave from her
factory job because she also suffers from a number of physical
problems.

Her concerns are now directed toward her children, who
also have undergone stress as a result of their sister's
death. The youngest child, seven, had been her sister's
playmate, and has felt the loss more keenly than the others.
This has been reflected in enuresis and difficulties in
school, both socially and academically. Mrs. L is aware of
this and has sought help with the school psychologist, whom
I have consulted.

Treatment is ongoing. Mrs. L still has dreams and
recurring thoughts that frequently cause depression, anxiety,
and sleeplessness. Nonetheless, she has picked up the pieces
of her life. I feel certain that with time she will continue
to make progress and accept the fact that she may always feel
some pain, but that her life and those of her loved ones can
continue and be meaningful.

CONCLUSION

The following is a list of concepts illustrated by the previous material:

Client-Focused Goals

1. To help clients work toward termination of their grief.

2. To determine the important priorities based on the needs of the clients.

3. To help clients discover a sense of purpose in their lives and futures.

4. To help clients learn more effective ways of coping with their lives.

5. To help clients plan their lives without their loved one.

6. To help support clients' creative efforts and to encourage them to find new and meaningful opportunities for socialization.

7. To try to draw in other family survivors in order to resolve their areas of guilt and doubt, and to enhance communication within the family.

8. To help clients focus on techniques that involve them in decision-making and the discovery of inner power.

Social Worker Focused Goals

1. To maintain a sympathetic and understanding attitude, but achieve separateness from their clients' grief.

2. To make an active commitment to learning grief counseling techniques and thanatological concepts.

3. For the practitioner in private practice, to establish periodic contact with others working in this field.

4. A bereaved client should not be turned away. Some of the most rewarding work can result from contact with this type of client. It need not be the exclusive specialty of the cancer clinic or hospital worker.

5. If one is going to accept responsibility for treating this type of person, it is important to

> offer support through extra office visits or by
> telephone calls when necessary.

The purpose of writing this paper has been to provide an
opportunity for me to discuss my role as a private social
worker in the treatment of the bereaved client. Working with
this type of client not only allows the worker to assist the
clients to cope with object loss, but also to help them plan
for their future. From my viewpoint, it has been most gratifying to help people find a sense of purpose in their lives
and to achieve a better sense of well-being.

REFERENCES

Miller, R.S. "Teaching Death and Dying Content in the Social
    Work Curriculum." In E.R. Prichard, J. Collard, B.A.
    Orcutt, A.H. Kutscher, I. Seeland, and N. Lefkowitz, eds.,
    Social Work with the Dying Patient and the Family, p. 290.
    New York: Columbia University Press, 1977.

Kübler-Ross, E. *On Death and Dying*, p. 206. New York:
    Macmillan, 1969.

20

The Financial Bridge: Counseling the Bereaved

Gerald Rosner

THE INSURANCE AGENT AS ULTIMATE INTERMEDIARY

Any physician in private practice can tell of patients
who had not been in for a check-up for years and then suddenly, almost in panic, called for an urgent appointment, not
because of the sudden appearance of ominous symptoms but
because of findings on an examination for life insurance.

Any lawyer in private practice can relate tales of
clients who had, for many years, resisted having their wills
drawn or revised or who, having had the drafts done, failed
to come in to sign the documents. Then, one day, out of
nowhere, the client calls with a sense of great urgency to
complete the transaction. Who was the *agent provocateur*?
The life insurance agent.

The agent is the eternal, the ultimate intermediary.
His constant lament is the necessity for follow-up. Why, he
keeps asking himself, won't people do, without prodding,
what is essential to their own best interests?

TRADITIONAL TRAINING METHODS

The agent's sales training is devoted to converting a
prospect for life insurance into a policyholder-client who
will, in turn, refer the agent to more prospects. Since the
agent's compensation is a commission based upon sales, he
must make decisions as to:

1. How much time can he afford to spend in develop-
   ing the case?

2. How much service can he afford to render his
   clients?

The answers to these questions are in part dictated by state laws which govern the maximum amount of commission an insurance company can pay an agent, in part by the attitudes and practices of the agency within whose framework the agent functions, but mostly by the agent himself who, like all professionals, is guided by his own sense of values and his own sense of obligation to his clients in particular and to society at large.

THE LIFE INSURANCE COMPANY'S ROLE

While the agent may and often does see his role as financial counselor, family and business advisor and catalyst, the view taken by the insurance company whose products the agent uses in solving a variety of financial problems is certainly less complex. It has a product to sell; it is a useful and necessary one; people will buy it out of self-interest; and the company will meet its obligations by paying off as promised. Somewhere along the way the company is supposed to make a profit and any activity in which the agent chooses to involve himself beyond that goal is his own business.

Hence, when the insurance company's obligation to pay the proceeds of a policy has been fulfilled, the agent's role as advisor and counselor continues to the surviving members of the family and business. It is quite natural for a widow, for example, to turn to her late husband's insurance man for financial counsel. Few agents indeed are capable of resisting such an appeal. But the agent must at this point question the basis of his own survival and should charge a fee for his time.

THE AGENT AS BRIDGE

Does the agent really have a vital function to perform after his client dies? We know that premortem estate planning is not only financially beneficial to the dying person, but to his survivors as well. It is also generally recognized that there are psychological benefits in having a listener, a third-party intermediary, to assist the dying person in putting his affairs in order.

It is my opinion that postmortem estate planning and financial counseling are equally important and beneficial. This is why the first two letters in my company's name are P.M., standing for either premortem or postmortem or for both. An actual case history where death was sudden and unexpected, where there was no opportunity for premortem planning, can serve as a valuable learning tool.

THE TRAUMA OF POSTMORTEM ESTATE PLANNING

Having achieved preeminence in his chosen field of academic medicine; having survived the Holocaust, raised a family and paid little attention to accumulating wealth, Dr. Y suddenly expired at the age of 63.

Funds had been set aside and earmarked for the completion of his two sons' professional education, which had already commenced. No special provision had been made for his 22-year-old daughter. All other property passed to the widow.

Mrs. Y, at one time a concert pianist, had devoted the better part of her adult life ministering to the needs of her husband and children. Her activities were solely within the family group, the classic *kinder, kirche, und küchen* pattern which predominated in middle European families prior to World War II.

Mrs. Y's trust in her husband was total and unquestioning. He made virtually every decision, no matter how minor. Matters of finance were entirely in his domain. Mrs. Y neither knew nor cared where the money for support came from nor where it went.

Her husband's sudden death threw Mrs. Y into hysterical panic. She had not the faintest notion of what to do or where to turn. Dr. and Mrs. Y had one close friend, a successful business man whose marketing skills were superior but whose familiarity with financial matters was limited. It was she who called me into the picture.

Drawers were emptied, checkbooks and savings accounts uncovered, mutual fund statements and cryptic receipts found in odd places. Dr. Y, a methodical researcher, was nonetheless a sloppy record keeper.

Examination of the scattered documents produced disheartening results: a pathetically meager estate. But I said nothing.

After the funeral and the period of mourning, Mrs. Y, exhausted by the frenzied pace of the week before, settled into a state of quiet desperation. She felt abandoned and lost, despite the supportive assurances of the children. The oldest of them (late 20s), a law student, tried in a touching way to play surrogate husband, a role doomed to failure from the start. The younger son, a second year medical student, withdrew rapidly and returned to his studies. The daughter's behavior was exemplary but rejected.

Mrs. Y needed a contemporary to lean on and I was there. She asked me to take over completely in all matters financial, work with a lawyer in settling the estate, and teach her how to manage whatever money there was.

I selected the older son as my associate. Together we rummaged through scores of folders and memoranda left by his father. Finally, we found what I was looking for and knew had to exist: a listing of group insurance, pension benefits, and Tax Sheltered Annuity participation furnished through his employer.

Dr. Y had been for 25 years research professor of medicine at one of the largest universities in the world. His salary was modest, his accumulated benefits huge by comparison. The group life insurance alone dwarfed Dr. Y's personal savings. Arrangements were being made to establish a library wing at the university's publications department. But not a single word emanated from the personnel department regarding the benefits due the widow.

I made a number of phone calls, received claim forms, searched endlessly for certificates, identifying numbers of various types and W-2 records. Dr. Y had prepared his own tax returns, had never used the services of an agent, broker, lawyer (except for his will), or accountant. He had been secretive and guarded in his conversation whenever money matters were mentioned. I began to hound the university personnel department in person and, after many false starts, finally found a sympathetic and knowledgeable employee who helped me piece together the fragments of Dr. Y's benefits program.

Because there were no confirming documents, however, each carrier had to be contacted by mail for verification of the amount of benefit and optional settlements available. As they were received, claim forms were filled and benefits commenced. Appropriate tax waivers were obtained and, as a complete picture emerged, I began to assemble and forward to the attorney information he would need for preparation of Form 706 (Estate Tax Return).

The law firm selected was a large and expensive one. By his own admission, the attorney calculated that I had done 80 percent of the leg work normally done by his firm in an estate of this size, and the legal fee was accordingly reduced from 5 percent of the gross estate to 1 percent, a saving of $12,000 to the estate.

As is often the case in postmortem estate planning, the next most cumbersome job after finding the assets was evaluating them. Two of the group benefits were contributory annuity plans which required first, ascertaining the amounts contributed by the decedent and then placing a date-of-death valuation on the balance.

Also included in the estate was some $14,000 of Series E bonds purchased in small denominations over a long period of time. The government prints tables of current valuation for Series E bonds which are, I am convinced, designed to induce blindness. We were literally forced to redeem the E bonds in order to obtain the proper valuation.

The resulting page 3 of the Estate Tax Return looks neat and trim and easy. Yet each of the entries required hours of laborious investigative effort, much of which could have been avoided through proper premortem planning.

Some of the insurances were put on interest option, others lumped out for investment in a variety of high yielding bonds and utility stocks. Mrs. Y and her family are enjoying a relatively comfortable style of living. She is slowly being taught how independently to manage her own affairs, though she continues to consult with me on matters great and small.

*   *   *

When close and distant relatives have departed after the funeral, who is left to console and advise the surviving family members?

Going it alone or relying on the advice of friends, relatives and acquaintances in matters of financial management will, in most cases, only add to the grief. Strength and firm guidance are needed. Ideally, the counselor who provides the guidance should be a person already known to the bereaved, already trusted, based on past relationships, and already familiar with the family's assets and style of living. The counselor could be the family lawyer or stockbroker or banker, but is most likely to be the life insurance agent. As part of the continuum, the agent should continue to serve as overall financial counselor, assisting in estate settlement and distribution, investing estate assets, and establishing budgetary priorities.

The financial counselor, no less than any other ministrant to the needs of the bereaved, must learn to recognize and accept the symptoms of normal as well as pathological mourning. Helping the bereaved to reorganize his or her life; helping the survivor redefine his or her role (e.g., no longer husband but widower; no longer one of a pair but a single person); assisting the survivor in learning a new skill as financial manager, leading to a feeling of independence--these are the agent's roles in the continuum. These services should be offered to and made acceptable to the bereaved.

Index

acceptance 9, 10, 11–14, 17; funeral directors' handling of 119, 121
addiction, drug 31, 32, 77, 78
adrenal cortex 55
adrenocorticotrophin hormone (ACTH) 55
Advances in Thanatology 110
Aisenberg, R., *The Psychology of Death* 110
"alarm" reaction 55, 56, 58
ambivalence: of the bereaved 12–14; in dying person 10–12, 20, 24, 25, 26
analgesic drugs 20, 31–32, 38
anger 3, 5, 10, 17; in the bereaved 29–30, 47; case study involving 25; funeral directors' handling of 119, 121–22
anticipatory grief 21–28; case studies of 23–27
antidepressants 24, 81
antipsychotics 78, 80
anxiety 22, 29, 47; aging and 86–87; in college students 62–65; in families of dying children 113
appetite, decreased 29, 138
"appropriate death" 31
arousal 27
"ars moriendi" 40
Art of Dying, The (Neale) 35
astrology 50
attachment, Bowlby's stage of 21

attention-seeking behavior 24
autonomy 26, 87
autopsy 4

B., Mrs. 134–35
Banuelos, Imelda 3–5
bargaining 10, 17, 20, 25; funeral directors' handling of 119, 121
Barrett, Virginia W. 85–90
Barten, H.H., *Brief Therapies* 110
Bartrop, R.W. 58
basilicas 51
Becker, Ernst, *The Denial of Death* 10–11
bereavement: acceptance and denial and 12–14; cancer resulting from stresses of 49–52; of families, *see* children; families, sons; spouses, bereaves; grief and 29–30; historical perspective on 48–53; loss and 11; planning for the elderly 88–89
Blank, H.R. 114
Bob 78–79
body preservation 35, 37–38
Bonica, John J. 30, 31, 32
Book of the Dead 49
Bowlby, J. 21
Brief Therapies (Barten) 110
brutalization 75, 76, 77, 78, 83
Buddhists 49, 53
Burton, C. 110

About the Editors and Contributors

Editors

DR. OTTO S. MARGOLIS Vice President for Academic Affairs, American Academy, McAllister Institute of Funeral Service.

HOWARD C. RAETHER Consultant (and formerly Executive Director), National Funeral Directors Association

DR. AUSTIN H. KUTSCHER President, The Foundation of Thanatology; Professor, Department of Psychiatry, College of Physicians and Surgeons, Columbia University

DR. SAMUEL C. KLAGSBRUN Medical Director, Four Winds Hospital; Associate Clinical Professor of Psychiatry, College of Physicians and Surgeons, Columbia University

DR. ERIC MARCUS Assistant Clinical Professor of Psychiatry, College of Physicians and Surgeons, Columbia University

DR. VANDERLYN R. PINE Professor of Sociology, State University of New York at New Paltz

DR. DANIEL J. CHERICO Assistant Professor and Coordinator, Department of Public Administration, Long Island University

LILLIAN G. KUTSCHER Publications Editor, The Foundation of Thanatology

Contributors

IMELDA BANUELOS, M.A. School Psychologist, Bethlehem, Pennsylvania

VIRGINIA W. BARRETT, R.N., M.Ed. Community Health Nursing Consultant, Columbia University Center for Geriatrics and Gerontology, and Long-Term Care Center

PAUL D. CHERULNIK, Ph.D. Associate Professor of Psychology, Susquehanna University, Susquehanna, Pennsylvania

JOAN M. DANTO, L.C.S.W. Social Work Practitioner, Fullerton, California

TAMARA FERGUSON, Ph.D. Adjunct Associate Professor of Sociology in Psychiatry, Wayne State University School of Medicine, Detroit, Michigan

JEROME F. FREDRICK, Ph.D. Director of Chemical Research, The Dodge Chemical Company, Bronx, New York

MAHLON S. HALE, M.D. Associate Professor and Director of Psychiatric Consultation Services, Health Sciences Center, University of Connecticut, Farmington, Connecticut

ROBERT A. HOGAN, Ph.D. Professor of Psychology, Illinois State University, Normal-Bloomington, Illinois

PAUL E. IRION, Ph.D. Professor of Theology, Lancaster Theological Seminary, Lancaster, Pennsylvania

GERALD A. LIENHART, M.S. Department of Psychology, Illinois State University, Normal-Bloomington, Illinois

JOANNE LoGIUDICE, D.A. Psychologist, Bethlehem, Pennsylvania

RAOUL L. PINETTE Funeral Service Director, Lewiston, Maine

JAMES T. QUATTLEBAUM, M.D. Honorary Member, Board of Directors, National Committee for the Treatment of Intractable Pain, Washington, D.C.

JUDITH H. QUATTLEBAUM President, National Committee for the Treatment of Intractable Pain, Washington, D.C.

GERALD ROSNER, Ch.F.C., C.L.U. President, PM Planning Co., New York, New York

STANLEY D. SAVICKI Simmons School of Mortuary Science, Utica, New York

VICTOR F. SCALISE, JR., Ph.D. President, New England Institute of Applied Arts and Sciences, Boston, Massachusetts

ARLENE SEGUINE, Ed.D. Associate Professor, Hunter College of the City University of New York, New York

VIRGINIA MONTERO SEPLOWIN, D.S.W. Right Human Relation Center, New York, New York

EGILDE SERAVALLI, Ph.D. Research Associate, Department of Anesthesia, Beth Israel Hospital and Medical Center, New York, New York

GARFIELD TOURNEY, M.D. Professor of Psychiatry, The University of Mississippi Medical Center, Jackson, Mississippi

RONALD E. TROYER Cincinnati College of Mortuary Science, Cincinnati, Ohio

SUMNER JAMES WARING, JR. Funeral Service Director, Fall River, Massachusetts